FAMILY CAREGIVERS AND DEPENDENT ELDERLY

SAGE HUMAN SERVICES GUIDES, VOLUME 38

SAGE HUMAN SERVICES GUIDES

a series of books edited by ARMAND LAUFFER and CHARLES GARVIN. Published in cooperation with the University of Michigan School of Social Work and other organizations.

A **SAGE** HUMAN SERVICES GUIDE **38**

FAMILY CAREGIVERS AND DEPENDENT ELDERLY

Minimizing Stress and Maximizing Independence

Dianne SPRINGER
Timothy H. BRUBAKER

Published in cooperation with the University of Michigan School of Social Work

SAGE PUBLICATIONS
Beverly Hills   London   New Delhi

PB595   11

For information address:

SAGE Publications, Inc.
275 South Beverly Drive
Beverly Hills, California 90212

SAGE Publications India Pvt. Ltd.
C-236 Defence Colony
New Delhi 110 024, India

SAGE Publications Ltd
28 Banner Street
London EC1Y 8QE, England

Printed in the United States of America

Library of Congress Cataloging in Publication Data
Springer, Dianne.
   Family caregivers and dependent elderly.

   (A Sage human services guide; 38)
   "Published in cooperation with the University of Michigan School of Social Work."
   Bibliography: p.
   1. Family social work—United States. 2. Aged—United States—Family relationships. 3. Aged—United States— Care and hygiene. 4. Aged—United States—Psychology. 5. Interpersonal communication—United States. I. Brubaker, Timothy H. II. Title. III. Series: Sage human services guides ; v. 38.
   HV1461.S67   1984   362.8′2   84-8245

ISBN 0-8039-2327-9 (pbk.)

SECOND PRINTING, 1985

1/17/86 *Becker + Tegler* 9·95

CONTENTS

ACKNOWLEDGMENTS

This book would not have been completed without the support of a number of individuals. We are grateful to Ellen MacDonald, Director of Nursing, Jewish Home for the Aged, Houston, Texas and Tilman Smith, Director of Programs and Studies for the Aging, Mennonite Board of Missions, Elkhart, Indiana for encouraging the "bridging of the gap between research and practice" in gerontology. Special thanks is given to Ellie Brubaker, Assistant Professor, Miami University, for providing support and insightful comments on every phase of this project. Also, Sherry Corbett, Associate Professor, Miami University, provided valuable comments on an earlier draft. Additional assistance was provided by Lynn Vesey. Gratitude is expressed to Carol Webb and Barbara Buckley for masterfully interpreting drafts and typing the manuscript. Recognition is given to the Family and Child Studies Center and the Department of Home Economics and Consumer Sciences for providing an environment in which this book could be completed.

PREFACE

Researchers and practitioners have a great deal to contribute to the field of gerontology. However, the perspectives and terminologies of each group tend to obstruct mutual understanding and communication. Generally, researchers write for other researchers. Their articles, reports, and presentations are filled with such terms as "hypotheses," "methodologies," "sampling procedures," and "generalized findings." On the other hand, practitioners are not as concerned about generalized findings as they are about specific techniques and skills to meet the individual needs of their elderly clients. Their terminology revolves around a different set of perspectives, theories, and concepts. With these differing perspectives and terminologies, practitioners may ignore the contributions of researchers and researchers may miss the contributions of practitioners.

The third group that is important includes the "clients" of the practitioners and the "subjects" of the researchers: older people and their families. This group is not interested in generalized findings or specific techniques; they desire information that will help them deal with the everyday problems they encounter. They want information that will be meaningful to their particular situation. Much of the information has been developed by the researchers but not translated to the older people and their clients. Many of the techniques of the practitioners are applicable to the older people and their families, but they have not been presented the techniques in a usable way.

This book was written to bridge the gaps among research, practice, and older people and their families. The primary focus is the caregiving responsibilities of family members who care for dependent older persons. The book seeks to translate "generalized findings" from research and "specific techniques" from practice for the family caregivers and their older family members. The information is research based. The emphasis is practice. The examples and exercises were designed to encourage families to deal with everyday problems in the caregiving situation.

There are three groups for whom this book was written. The first and foremost group includes individuals who care for dependent older persons. In most instances these are family members who provide an extraordinary amount of care and support to dependent older family members. They may provide care in the home of the older person or they may reside in the same household as the older person. These households may include a number of generations or only one generation. There are a variety of settings in which individuals provide care for dependent older persons. This book includes information to help caregivers understand the aging processes, stresses and problems associated with the caregiving role, and ways to consider changes that might lessen the difficulty in fulfilling the demands of caregiving. There are exercises and an Action Plan to encourage caregivers in the application of the information presented.

The second group for whom this book was written includes practitioners who work with family caregivers and older persons. These practitioners may be social workers, nurses, physical therapists, psychologists, clergy, or other professionals who provide services to dependent older persons. As practitioners deal with the concerns and frustrations of family caregivers, they need to understand more about the aging processes and/or the caregiving role. This book translates the research information so that practitioners can use this material. Most of the exercises can be used by practitioners to help family caregivers examine the caregiving role more closely. The Action Plan can be used to assist caregivers to understand better the interface between informal and formal support systems.

The third group includes support groups of caregivers. In some communities groups of caregivers have developed linkages to support one another. Some caregivers may wish to establish such groups. This book can be used as the basis of a discussion session and encourages group members to examine carefully the caregiving role and the various supports available in fulfilling this role. The exercises can be shared with the group, and the Action Plan can be shared with other group members.

The primary objective of this book, regardless of the audience, is to maximize the independence of the dependent older person and minimize the stressful situations experienced by the caregiver. It is our hope that this book will strengthen the family relationships of the caregivers and dependent older persons.

At the end of each chapter a "Suggestions for Practice" section is included. This section provides a few activities that can be initiated by service professionals and that can encourage caregivers to examine closely the caregiving role and to identify ways to help the elderly. The activities are based on the assumption that service professionals will be working with caregivers in a group or individual setting. The suggestions are only a beginning; service providers are urged to develop other activities that might be applicable to their particular community.

Chapter 1

INTRODUCTION

CASE 1

Sue is a 40-year-old housewife. Besides chauffeuring her very active 13-year-old son and 15-year-old daughter to extracurricular school activities, maintaining the household responsibilities, and providing emotional support to her husband who is currently facing a stressful job situation, she has begun caring for her 70-year-old widowed father. Her father had a stroke recently. After her father's stroke, Sue dropped the two college courses she was taking so that she could visit him regularly and help with his rehabilatation in the hospital. Upon his release from the hospital Sue's father moved into her home for an indefinite length of time. This seemed to be the only option, with the exception of relocation to a nursing home. No one wanted to place Sue's father in a nursing home. Sue's brother and sister live out of town and are unable to provide physical care for their father. They offered to provide some financial support to Sue if she would care for their father. It has been several months since Sue's father moved into her home. She finds herself overwhelmed with the competing demands of her husband, children, and father.

CASE 2

Emily is 73 years of age. Her 79-year-old husband, Joe, is homebound due to complications with diabetes. He is almost blind and six months ago had his right leg amputated. Emily is providing care for Joe at home. Also, she is not well herself. She is very weak and suffers from hypertension. Some of the equipment she uses to take care of Joe is more for her benefit than for his. For example, she uses a mechanical lift to help Joe move from his bed to a chair. He would be able to get out of bed himself if he had a little physical support, but Emily is too weak to provide that support. Emily's doctor is very concerned about her health. He is afraid that Emily will suffer a disabling stroke if she does not slow down. Emily and Joe have no living children or grandchildren. She does not know where to turn.

CASE 3

Sam's 85-year-old father died three years ago. Two weeks after his father's death, Sam moved his 83-year-old mother to the home he and his wife share. Sam was concerned about the grief his mother was feeling and thought he could help her by introducing her to new people and experiences. With that thought in mind, it seemed appropriate to move his mother to his community, 50 miles away from where his father and mother had lived for the past 45 years. Since the move, Sam notices that his mother sometimes wants to talk about her husband's death. When this happens, Sam quickly changes the subject to more cheerful topics. Though Sam's mother is physically able to get around and used to enjoy going to a variety of places, she now wants to stay inside most of the time. She is not interested in meeting new people or accompanying Sam and his wife to the activities they enjoy. Sam notices his mother is becoming more and more withdrawn and depressed. He wishes his mother could just "snap out of it." If she does not, he feels he will need to consider placing her in a nursing home.

WHO ARE THE DEPENDENT ELDERLY?

In these cases, Joe, Sue's father, and Sam's mother represent the small segment of the elderly population that gerontologists use a variety of adjectives to describe: "impaired," "disabled," "frail," or "dependent." There is no good word to describe this group of older persons. "Impaired," "disabled," and "frail" depict an image of *physically* handicapped persons. However, the group of elderly who need caregivers are not *all* physically handicapped. This group includes persons with economic, social, and psychological dependencies. Therefore, the term "dependent elderly" is often used to represent these persons. They are no longer able to take complete control of their lives and for some reason need major assistance from other persons to perform activities associated with daily living.

Although we use the term "dependent elderly" in this book, we do so cautiously. As noted above, this term can be misleading. These persons may be dependent on others for certain things, some of which may be major, but they are not *totally* dependent. Furthermore, we are all dependent on others in order to function in our society. For example, we depend on others to provide us with news about national and world events. We depend on farmers to grow food for our consumption. We depend on medical doctors to heal us. It is not bad to be dependent. On the other hand, our emotional well-being is enhanced if we have a certain amount of control, or independence, over our lives. Although some persons may no longer be able to assume as much control over their lives as they once did, it is essential to their emotional well-being that they assume as much control or independence as they are physically and mentally able. It is important for caregivers and others who relate to these older people to create environments in which their maximum level of independency can be attained.

It may be helpful to visualize the concept of dependence as a continuum:

dependent   independent

$$\vdash \!\!\!—————————————————————————\!\!\! \dashv$$

An older person may be anywhere along this continuum depending on the skill he or she may be trying to achieve. For example, a person may be physically dependent, mentally independent, socially dependent, and financially independent. Older persons who are dependent may require another individual to provide care for them. *It is our belief that a caregiver's objective should be to provide an environment where a "dependent" older person is encouraged to move to his or her greatest possible degree of independency in as many facets of life as possible.*

TO WHAT EXTENT ARE FAMILIES INVOLVED?

In the case studies at the beginning of this chapter, Sue, Emily, and Sam, like many others, are involved in the care of their dependent elderly family members and dispel the myth of the "abandoned" or "dumped" elderly (Brubaker, 1983; Brody, 1981; Brandwein and Postoff, 1980; Hamrick and Blazer, 1980; Ward, 1978). Research has shown that families are financially, physically, and emotionally involved with their older members to the extent that they can be (Branch and Jette, 1983; Brody, 1978,1981; Cantor, 1979, 1983; Shanas, 1979a, 1979b; White House Conference on Aging Final Report, 1981; Silverman et al., 1977; Soldo and Myllyluoma, 1983). Even when assistance from outside agencies is necessary, the family persists as a primary source of help to its elderly members (Cantor, 1979; Shanas, 1979b; Cicirelli, 1981; Brody et al., 1978). A recent summary of research on family involvement in later life concluded that "a viable family network exists for many older people and family relationships in later life are important to *both* older people and other family members" (Brubaker, 1983: 18). We can add that *family members provide an extraordinary amount of assistance to their older family members.*

The family role seems to become even more important when older family members become more dependent (White House Conference on Aging Final Report, 1981). Using 1975 survey data of the noninstitutionalized population aged 65 years and older, Shanas (1979a) reports that approximately 3% of the total sample were classified as bedfast and an additional 7% as homebound. These persons constitute twice the proportion of older adults who are institutionalized. These data indicate that the majority of the sick and frail elderly were not in institutions in 1975; most were living in their own homes, and a small portion lived in homes with other family members. For this small group of families, stress may develop within the intergenerational households. Brubaker and Brubaker (1981) discuss the inter- and intrafamily resources that are important in dealing with stress in intergenerational households.

For those who were institutionalized after age 85 or older, 42% had lived in private residences just prior to their move. This suggests that a large percentage of family members served as caregivers as long as it was possible to keep their older family members in the community. Brody et al. (1978) cite 1972 data from the National Health Statistics indicating that 80% of all home health care for the dependent elderly is provided by family caregivers. Two conclusions can be drawn from these studies. *First, family caregivers are not alone (at least in numbers) in the caregiving role.* Second, *family caregivers are pivotal in determining whether an older dependent person will remain in the community or will be institutionalized* (Brody et al., 1978; Palmore, 1976; Townsend, 1965).

WHO ARE THE CAREGIVERS?

Currently, the majority of caregivers of the dependent elderly are spouses or adult children. These caregivers are supplemented by other family members (Soldo and Myllyluoma, 1983; Bell, 1973). If the dependent person's spouse is living, he or she will usually serve as the primary caregiver for as long as possible. If both members of the elderly couple are dependent or if the elderly parent is alone, a middle-aged child is likely to become the primary caregiver (Rathbone-McCuan, 1976). Recently, Cantor (1983) reported that nearly as many children were primary caregivers as spouses.

In the United States, the primary family caregivers have traditionally been women. Steinmetz and Amsden (1983) report that 94% of 104 caregivers in their sample were female, and Cantor (1983) found that 70% of the 111 caregivers in her sample were women. The caregiver in the elderly couple is most often the wife, given that women generally live longer than men and are most often younger than their husbands (Shanas, 1979b). Adult children serving in the primary caregiver role usually tend to be daughters or daughters-in-law of the older dependent person (Frankfather et al., 1981). Thus *the caregivers are most likely to be women and will either be the spouse or daughter of the dependent person.*

Recent increases in the proportion of women working have resulted in the majority of middle-aged wives, daughters, and daughters-in-law being employed outside their homes (Brody, 1981). These women, as never before, are being asked to assume roles of paid workers *and* caregivers. In most cases, these roles are being added to their other roles of wives, homemakers, mothers, and grandmothers (Brody, 1981). Consequently, physical and emotional pressures may be increasing as middle-aged women assume both caregiving and working roles.

With the increase in longevity, a larger number of older people have become caregivers. The example of Emily at the beginning of this chapter is not uncommon. As people live to be 80-90 years old, they receive care from family members who are elderly themselves. Not all of these older caregivers are spouses or siblings. Frequently the dependent older person's children, who are more than 60 years old, assume the caregiving responsibilities.

FOR WHAT REASONS
DO PEOPLE BECOME CAREGIVERS?

If we were to ask caregivers to explain why they are caring for an older family member, we would likely get as many different answers as there are caregivers. The literature suggests several common reasons for persons assuming these responsibilities. Some feel an obligation to care for their older family member (Frankfather et al., 1981). Perhaps some caregivers want to repay their father or mother for all he or she has done in the past. Others fear a nursing home placement for their older family member and prefer to care for him or her at home. Some spouses view caregiving in the home as a literal and practical interpretation of the "in sickness and in health" vow they pledged when they married. Others may have been motivated by guilt feelings for something that happened in their past relationship with the older person and may try to compensate by serving as a caregiver. *We believe that it is important for the caregiver to be sensitive to the reasons he or she has chosen to assume the role of caregiver.*

WHAT IS NEEDED TO
SUPPORT FAMILY CAREGIVERS?

Although the literature has shown that families are a voluntary and viable resource to their dependent elderly members, *it appears that most family members need help in learning to assume a caregiver role* (Safford, 1980). No preparation is given to people for the kinds of stresses and duties they must deal with in the caregiving role. Think back to the earlier illustrations and the frustrations and stresses both the caregiver and older relative must have felt.

Today when someone is employed, he or she can usually expect to be given a job description to help understand how to carry out his or her new tasks effectively. Also, we have an understanding of certain societal expectations for persons assuming roles such as mother, father, brother, or sister. Although these expectations are not formalized in a job description, people generally know something of what others expect of them in their particular role. But what is the job description or role of the caregiver? There are few societal guidelines for the role of caregiver to the elderly (Getzel, 1981). Caregivers may not know how much care is appropriate to give, if certain feelings are appropriate, or which of their own needs may be appropriate to meet. There is no formal way to determine whether they are overdoing or underdoing their tasks. This uncertainty may be a source of stress for the caregivers (Getzel, 1981).

In addition to access to job descriptions, workers often have access to some type of training to prepare them for their jobs. Again, this is usually unavailable for caregivers. Sometimes caregivers experience frustrations because they know little about the aging process and therefore do not know how to respond to behavioral changes in their older family member. The following illustrates some of the sources of stress that enter into the family caregiving relationship:

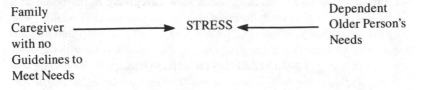

The importance of providing support for family caregivers has been noted by service providers, gerontological researchers, and family caregivers (Hartford and Parsons, 1982; Archbold, 1980; Silverman and Brahce, 1979; Brandwein and Postoff, 1980; Safford, 1980; Crossman et al., 1981; Zarit, 1980; Fengler and Goodrich, 1979; Rathbone-McCuan, 1976; Brody, 1981). Mutual support groups of persons sharing a similar caregiving experience are one external support that has been found to strengthen successfully the role of the caregiver. These groups often have two primary purposes: to offer emotional support to its members and to provide didactic material relevant to the caregiving role. This didactic material may include information on the aging process, formal and informal resources available to the caregiver, and information to promote a deeper understanding of communication and relationship patterns (McCubbin et al., 1980; Hartford and Parsons, 1982).

Support groups have been found to reduce the social and emotional isolation experienced by caregivers. The peer support expands the support network for caregivers and addresses needs that cannot be met by family, friends, or formal support systems. The mutual support and recognition caregivers gain have been found to have a positive effect on their self-esteem (Crossman et al., 1981). It is important for the adult caregiver to have an opportunity to explore his or her feelings about caregiving responsibilities and limitations, as well as to learn about available resources, before a time of crisis (Hausman, 1979).

FOCUS OF THE BOOK

This book provides adult caregivers with information about aging and caregiving relationships in later life. The content can be useful to individual caregivers and support groups of caregivers. Questions and exercises are included to encourage self-examination of the caregiving role. It is our hope that this book will provide information to equip adult caregivers to develop a job description. The primary focus of the job description should include *maximizing the independence of the dependent older person and minimizing the stress experienced by the caregiver and the caregiver's family.*

ORGANIZATION OF THE BOOK

The book is organized to present information about the caregiving role as well as aspects that may enhance the relationship between the caregiver and dependent older person. The caregiver may be a family member or a close friend. The caregiver may be female or male. In any case, the material is organized to equip the caregiver with knowledge about the aging process, stressful situations, and ways to cope with the difficulties related to the caregiving role.

Many caregivers are not aware of the changes an older person experiences as a result of typical aging processes. Chapter 2 is an overview of physical and psychological changes associated with getting older. Also, attention will be directed toward some of the emotional needs of a person who is aging.

Potentially stress-producing situations are the focus of Chapters 3 and 4. Topics include the ambiguous role of the caregiver, health problems of both the dependent older person and the caregiver, financial aspects, decision-making, changes in family routines, role shifts, competing demands, family conflicts, behavioral and mood changes in the older person, and emotional responses the caregiver may feel. We will also discuss ways to relieve some of the stress brought about by these situations.

In Chapters 5 and 6 we will look at communication skills: communication, communicating within a family context, reality orientation, and the use of life review in communication. Exercises are suggested that can enhance communication skills.

As we noted, families and friends provide a great deal of support to dependent older persons. "Informal support system" is the concept used to categorize this type of support. Chapter 7 focuses on the informal supports that may be available to caregivers. We will discuss how other family members, friends, and neighbors can assist with caregiving responsibilities. An exercise is described that encourages caregivers to look specifically at their own informal support systems.

In Chapter 8 we will focus on formal supports that may be available to the caregiver. These include agencies and service providers who offer services to support the caregivers' responsibilities. A unique Action Plan is presented to give the caregiver an opportunity to gain access to his or her needs and resources. In the Action Plan the caregiver is asked to list friends, family members, neighbors, and community service agencies who offer support and assistance in caring for older family member.

SUGGESTIONS FOR PRACTICE

1. Form a group of caregivers and discuss various aspects of the caregiving role. To determine the knowledge level of caregivers, ask each caregiver to complete the Caregiver Knowledge Exercise discussed in Chapter 9. If the group wants more information, organize meetings to discuss the various chapters in this book.

2. Encourage caregivers to examine their feelings about caregiving. Who is responsible to provide assistance to a dependent older family member? Who should be the primary caregiver? To what degree should other family members help? Urge the caregivers to consider their expectations about their role as well as their feelings toward the dependent older person.

Chapter 2

AN OVERVIEW OF THE
AGING PROCESS

Key Questions

1. Has anyone ever died of old age?
2. What are some general changes in appearance that take place as we grow old?
3. What are some changes that take place within the body?
4. How many older people have health problems?
5. What may happen to our minds as we grow older?
6. How do emotional needs change as we grow older?

CASE 1

Mrs. Smith is 91 years old. Three years ago, at the age of 88, she underwent major surgery for the removal of a malignancy. This was her first hospitalization since the birth of her last child 50 years earlier. One week following her surgery she was discharged to her son-in-law and daughter's home for recuperation. After staying three weeks with them, she moved back into her own home. She lives alone and remains active. Her doctor has given her a clean bill of health since her surgery. She performs all routine household tasks without assistance. Even though she is slightly stooped, she is able to exercise three afternoons each week by walking around the neighborhood. She is ready to go out with friends at a moment's notice. Each summer she and her 65-year-old daughter travel extensively for two or three weeks. Her primary physical impairment is a moderate hearing loss.

CASE 2

Mrs. Jones recently celebrated her sixty-third birthday. Last year she and her husband celebrated her birthday eating dinner at their favorite restaurant. This year her mobility has been so severely limited by arthritis that she was forced to celebrate her birthday at home. Mrs. Jones, now very stooped and in severe pain, requires the use of a walker. Although she is on medication, nothing seems to relieve her constant pain. She has lost so much strength in her hands and arms that she is no longer able to perform minor household responsibilities. Mr. Jones does all the cooking, cleaning, and laundry.

Does it seem that we may have mistakenly switched these women's ages? It would seem to make more sense for the 91-year-old woman to be the one experiencing difficulty with mobility and the 63-year-old person to be active. Although many people generally believe that the older person should have more physical problems, that is not always the case. These women highlight the complexity and uniqueness of the aging process. They also illustrate both typical age-related changes and disease processes in later life. We will discuss such changes and diseases in this chapter.

Very likely our past and current experiences with older persons influence our understanding and feelings about the aging process, as well as how we relate to older people (Brubaker and Powers, 1976; Brubaker and Barresi, 1979; Barresi and Brubaker, 1979). You may know older people who are living independently. However, as a caregiver or service provider who intensely relates to an older person who has experienced enough problems to cause him or her to relinquish some independence, you may be tempted to equate his or her dependency with old age. You may believe his or her situation is hopeless and an inevitable result of getting older. And your lack of knowledge about typical aging processes may encourage you to perpetuate his or her and your own frustration. You may develop fears about your own aging. Many of these fears may be unfounded. For these reasons it is important to be aware of the potential losses, retentions, and gains of aging and to make a distinction between so-called typical age-related changes and disease processes.

This chapter provides a brief overview of the aging process. In a general way we will look at what may happen to our bodies, minds, and emotions as we grow older. An in-depth exploration of these areas is beyond the scope of this chapter. More detailed information about specific physical, psychological, or emotional aspects related to an older family member can be obtained from a geriatric nurse practitioner, physician, geriatric social worker, or psychologist. An additional reading list is presented at the end of the chapter, and a simulation exercise is presented to help you understand more fully some of the sensory losses an older dependent person may be experiencing.

HAS ANYONE EVER DIED
OF OLD AGE?

Have you ever been told someone "died of old age"? Unfortunately, some people believe this happens. However, people *do not* die from "old age." Old age is *not* a disease. Nor is being *old* equivalent to being *sick*. Some "old" people are sick, but so are some "young" people. Not *all* "young" people are sick, just as not all "old" people are sick. Too often medical personnel pass off an older person's physical complaint as due to old age and do not investigate to determine if the situation can be treated and reversed (Butler, 1975). *At times, doctors need to be challenged about their diagnoses* of older patients' physical complaints. An older family member's aches and pains may very well be eliminated with proper medical attention.

Think back to the two case examples at the beginning of this chapter. Mrs. Smith had surgery for a malignancy. She did not have the malignancy because she was old. Once the malignancy was removed, she was able to continue with her life in much the same way she had before she got sick. Her moderate hearing loss is a normal age-related change. All persons, if they live long enough, will experience a loss in hearing sensitivity (Rockstein and Sussman, 1979). Similarly, her slightly stooped posture is a normal age-related change due to general muscular weakness and loss of vertebral discs (Rakowski and Hickey, 1976). On the other hand, Mrs. Jones's stooped posture is due to the disease of arthritis. Her posture has nothing to do with her physical age.

Sometimes it is difficult to distinguish typical age-related changes from disease processes. As a person becomes older, the changes that take place in his or her body may increase vulnerability to disease. The typical age-related changes and the disease may interact with each other and speed the person's aging. The person's environment and lifestyle may further speed or retard the aging process. In short, *"aging" is a highly individualistic and complex process.*

WHAT CHANGES IN OUR BODIES
AS WE GROW OLDER?

Caution is needed when talking about the changes that take place in our bodies as we age. Some of the changes we talk about may affect everyone if they live long enough. However, the extent to which these changes take place will vary for each person. Other changes we talk about may occur in some people but not in others (Rockstein and Sussman, 1979). None of us ages in the same way. One person's hair may become gray at an earlier age than another's. One person may be less ambulatory at age 85 than another. Your family member, at age 80 years, may hear much better than your neighbor's older relative who is only 70 years old.

Not only do we age differently from each other, but our body organs age at different rates (Rockstein and Sussman, 1979). The stomach of an older person aged 75 years may function similar to other "healthy" 75 year-old stomachs. However, the person's heart may resemble the heart of a "healthy" 60-year-old. On the other hand, the aging of one organ may affect the efficiency of another organ. For example, the changes in the respiratory system are closely connected to changes in other systems of the body (Gilbert, 1977). This means *we need to keep in mind individual differences as we talk about age-related changes in general.*

Changes Without and Within the Body

Let us think of some of the signs that indicate a person is growing older. The majority of things you think about have to do with changes in general appearance: graying hair, wrinkled skin, age spots, or stooped posture. Most likely you have noticed these changes in your older family member, and possibly in yourself, over the years. Although the outward signs of aging are what we probably are most familiar with, they are simply an indication of what is taking place inside our bodies (Gilbert, 1977).

One way to understand the processes of internal aging in a general and rather simplistic way is to think of the body as a "cell manufacturing company" (Gilbert, 1977). We became the owner of this "company " at the moment of conception. Each cell the company produces has its own lifespan. As long as the "workers" are able to produce new cells faster than the old cells die, aging takes the form of growth. This kind of "production" takes place in the younger years. As we get older, the cell production workers tend to slow down so that the old cells die more rapidly than the workers are able to replace them. Growth is replaced by loss of reserves and decreased efficiency of various organ functioning. This, along with tissue changes, redistribution of fats, and water and chemical factors are partly responsible for changes within the body. Disease and environmental stress add to the rate of changes taking place (Gilbert, 1977).

Let us look briefly at our heart, respiratory, and sensory systems to see what changes may take place as we grow older.

The Cardiovascular System. This system includes the heart and blood vessels. Although some changes occur with age, these are often complicated by disease, changes from other systems, and injury (Gilbert, 1977). The valves do not function as well as they did and the rhythm becomes irregular. The artery walls tend to become thicker, brittle, and disorganized (Gilbert, 1977). These changes may lead to circulatory problems, high blood pressure, and heart disease.

Heart disease causes the majority of activity limitation and is the most common cause of death for persons 65 years and over. This disease needs to be taken seriously. Prevention through appropriate diet, exercise, and stress reduction is important.

Respiratory System. The respiratory system includes the lungs and air passageways (Rockstein and Sussman, 1979). The respiratory system, more than any other bodily system, suffers from environmental attacks such as air pollution and smoking. The "true" age-related changes in this system cause decreased breathing capacity in the older person (Rockstein and Sussman, 1979). These changes do not impair everyday functioning for most people until old age, but they do cause the body to respond less efficiently to prolonged stresses (Rakowski and Hickey, 1976).

Diseases of the respiratory system include emphysema, pneumonia, and tuberculosis. Emphysema is found more often in persons who smoke heavily and/or live in areas with high levels of air pollution (Rockstein and Sussman, 1979). Pneumonia is an especially high-risk disease for older bedridden persons. Immobility also may cause blood clots that block the circulation in blood vessels of the lung. This may be fatal. If an older family member is bedridden, be sure to contact a doctor to see how you can prevent blood clots. Many respiratory diseases are not unique to older persons but are more often fatal among older persons (Rockstein and Sussman, 1979).

The Sensory System. Sensory organs are perhaps the most important part of the body. These are the organs we rely on most heavily as we communicate with others and as we relate to and adjust to our environment

(Gilbert, 1977). Our senses enable us to see our family, friends, trees, flowers and other things in our world; to read; to hear beautiful music, traffic on a busy street, people speak to us, and other sounds of our environment; to smell pleasant odors or odors indicating danger, such as smoke; to enjoy good food; and to experience the sensations of softness, roughness, heat, and cold.

Our senses diminish as we grow older. In general, "aging" eyes need more light and more time to adapt to both light and darkness (Neuhaus and Neuhaus, 1982). And the lenses of the eye tend to yellow so that the colors of violet, blue, and green become more difficult to distinguish (Atchley, 1980). Table 2.1 presents common vision problems and ways to help an older person cope with these problems.

"Aging" ears are less able to hear higher pitches and have difficulty discriminating two sounds produced in close succession (Rockstein and Sussman, 1979). Approximately 30% of people 65 years and older have hearing losses that interfere with their communication. The changes may come so gradually that the older person unknowingly makes slight adjustments to compensate for the loss. He or she may not actually become aware of the disability until it is extreme. Do you, as a caregiver, ever find yourself shouting at the person you are caring for and wonder why he or she is not aware of how deaf he or she is? *A hearing loss, more than any other sensory loss, tends to isolate an older person from society.* This isolation may be of such intensity that the older person shows symptoms of paranoia (Rockstein and Sussman, 1979). It is important for a caregiver to find ways to include his or her hearing-impaired family member in family interactions so he or she does not feel isolated.

The third sense is taste. The number of taste buds decline with age, so that the ability to taste sugar and salt declines, although the tastes of of sour and bitter remain the same. (Waters et al., 1980). In order to make their food taste the way it used to, older people may increase their use of sugar and salt. These increased amounts are usually unhealthy. A caregiver may be able to increase an older family member's interest in eating by planning attractive, nutritious meals and increasing opportunities for social contact at mealtime.

The sense of smell contributes almost as much to the "taste" of food as do taste buds (Rockstein and Sussman, 1979). Also, smell declines with age and may contribute to lack of interest in food (Neuhaus and Neuhaus, 1982). This sensory loss may be extremely hazardous if an older person is unable to detect odors of dangerous gases and smoke from fires (Rockstein and Sussman, 1979).

The sense of touch diminishes with age. Older people are less resistant to temperature change (Neuhaus and Neuhaus, 1982). If caution is not taken,

TABLE 2.1
Vision Difficulties and Interventions

A. Recognizing Vision Difficulties

1. Coordination difficulties: Any behavior that relates to the person's ability to find and handle objects could indicate visual problems. Examples include difficulties in walking, buttoning a button, or finding food on a plate.

2. Positioning objects in direct line of vision: A person may use his or her hands to "feel for" objects placed outside the line of vision. Because he or she can't see those objects, he or she may fumble or spill them.

3. Squinting of eyes in attempt to see things more clearly.

4. Color selections: When a person consistently selects brighter colored object in contrast to duller ones.

5. Uncontrolled eye movements: Eye movements that seem to be uncoordinated and not directed toward a particular object.

6. Depth perception: In reaching for objects, will constantly overshoot or undershoot the object.

7. Inability to copy: Can't look at an object and draw it accurately.

8. General: The older person with a vision problem may be unable to recognize other people and he or she may miss handshakes because he or she can't see the hand. Also may not be able to distinguish an object from its background, or may have difficulty moving about because of inability to see objects in his or her path.

B. Interventions for Visual Impairments

1. Place objects in the person's visual field (i.e., glasses of water, silverware, medicines).

2. Label objects: Large lettering on such things as telephone, doors and hallways, medicines, and even clothing can facilitate the older person's adaptation to the environment and maintain his or her independence.

3. Simplify the visual field: The more cluttered a space is, the more difficult it is for the visually handicapped person to identify the correct object. Remove objects from person's visual field that aren't necessary.

4. Consistently place objects: Don't move or rearrange objects so that they are difficult for person to locate (i.e., always put person's shoes in the same location).

5. Use of bright colors: Color-code objects such as faucet tops, hallways, medicines, etc.

6. Give prewarning: Visual hallucinations are quite common among the elderly. In approaching a visually impaired older person, if one moves too rapidly or unexpectedly, fear can be unintentionally aroused in the person. Announcing to an older person what you are going to do gives him or her advance warning of your actions and prevents misunderstanding of the situation (i.e., don't move the person in a wheelchair without telling him or her where he or she is being taken).

(continued)

TABLE 2.1 Continued
___

7. Encourage use of other sensory mechanisms: Visually impaired person may have to touch, smell, or taste objects in order to be able to make proper identification.

8. Offer to read those things the older person can no longer read himself or herself.

As an older person experiences loss in vision, he or she may be hesitant to admit it or to seek help. The caregiver needs to be aware of this and help the person understand changing vision.

___

Reprinted with permission from M. Ernst and H. Shore, *Sensitizing People to the Processes of Aging: The In-Service Educator's Guide.* Denton: Center for Studies in Aging, North Texas State University, 1975.

this can cause an abnormally low body temperature (hypothermia) when exposed to cold temperatures and heat stroke (hyperthermia) following exposure to high temperatures.

Because we rely so heavily on our senses in order to adapt to our environment, it may be helpful for a caregiver to experience sensory losses similar to those experienced by an older family member. At the end of this chapter is a Sensory Loss Exercise. Caregivers are encouraged to simulate the sensory losses their older family members are experiencing so as to increase their own sensitivity to some of the barriers their dependent relatives face with these losses.

HOW MANY OLDER PEOPLE HAVE HEALTH PROBLEMS?

We have discussed both age-related changes and disease processes. How many older people have health problems? In light of the fact that all caregivers relate to someone who has enough health problems to require regular assistance, it may seem as though the majority of older people require assistance because they have health difficulties. However, this is not the case. *Approximately 80% of older adults who are 65 years old and older have adequate health to live independently* (Waters et al., 1980). Many of these people may have a chronic (or long-term) health problem, such as visual or hearing impairments, high blood pressure, diabetes, or arthritis. However, their health problems are not disabling to the point that they can no longer care for themselves at home.

Approximately 20%, or 3-4 billion, older people need outside help in order to manage (Waters et al., 1980). These people are often referred to as the "frail" or "dependent elderly" and include many of the persons being cared for by family caregivers. *It is important to keep in mind that with the physical changes accompanying aging, older persons do become more susceptible to illness.* Preventive health measures such as diet and exercise and early detection of illnesses can help an older person remain independent. Regular medical exams are important for an older person.

The literature suggests that even though physical changes accompany old age, most older people are able to cope well because the changes are gradual enough that they are able to make necessary psychological and emotional adjustments (Waters et al., 1980). Let us spend some time looking at psychological and emotional changes that may accompany aging.

WHAT CHANGES CAN BE EXPECTED IN OUR INTELLECTUAL CAPACITIES?

Intelligence

Common stereotypes about aging, which relate to the use of our minds, frequently prompt people to associate decrements or losses with aging. For example, the saying "you can't teach an old dog new tricks" implies that an older person has lost some intelligence and ability to learn. This is not true. Studies that have compared the same people over time have shown very little change in intelligence (Atchley, 1980). These studies do show that intelligence drops significantly just before someone dies, but not until then. *Older persons are able to learn new things.* They usually need more time to learn, but they definitely have the ability. And older people have an easier time learning things that have some meaning for them (Neuhaus and Neuhaus, 1982). If they see no purpose for something, they may not exert as much energy to attempt to learn it. This may be something to remember if a caregiver is trying to teach a new skill to the person he or she is caring for. If the older person seems to refuse stubbornly to learn the skill, it may be because he or she does not see the value of it. The caregiver should talk to the older family member about his or her feelings regarding the task and explain the reasons the new skill can have meaning. Perhaps the caregiver and older person can come to a joint decision as to whether it is a skill worth learning. As the caregiver talks with the older person, it is important to remain open to the possibility that the new skill might not be worth learning from the older person's perspective.

Obviously, a person's health will affect his or her interest and/or willingness to learn something. If someone is experiencing a great deal of pain and discomfort, he or she may not be motivated to learn something no matter how meaningful it may seem.

Memory

Another stereotype in our society equates forgetfulness with old age (Rakowski and Hickey, 1976). A young person can forget something and it is attributed to absent-mindedness or "having a lot on his or her mind". An older person can forget the same thing and it is associated with old age and/or senility. *Contrary to popular belief, some older persons never experience memory loss. Persons who use their memories throughout their lifetimes tend to keep them well into old age* (Atchley, 1980). However, memory loss may occur to some extent in older persons. When memory loss does occur, it appears to occur more often with things learned recently than with events of long ago (Atchley, 1980).

A dependent older person may forget something the caregiver told him or her two hours ago but can easily recall the minutest details of life on the farm 65 years ago. Studies (Atchley, 1980) have shown that as one ages, one can retain things better that one has heard than things one has seen. *If one has both heard and seen something, the retention is better yet.* Therefore, if a caregiver wants to tell something to an older family member and wants him or her to remember it, it may be helpful both to explain the information and to show a few related visual cues. For example, in order to help an older relative remember appointments, it might be helpful to not only tell him or her about the appointments but also to point out the day on a calendar.

One of the most widely supported theories about memory loss is that new material interferes with the recall of old material (Atchley, 1980). As a person ages, he or she learns more and more new material that can interfere with other material. *It takes an older person longer to "sift" through his or her "memory bank."* Remote and old memory is not easily forgotten because it has been a part of the person's experiences for a longer period of time.

Life Review

A final stereotype we will review in this chapter is that older people often live in the past. This is a healthy activity for most older people that involves review and integration of life experiences. Robert Butler (1968), a geriatric physician, found that persons attempt to evaluate their past in order to accept their lives with both its successes and its failures. Additionally, persons engaged in life review attempt to think and feel through what they will do with the time that is left to them. Thus life review is an attempt to put one's life in order (Butler, 1968).

Beyond this, an older person's storytelling of the "good old days" may be nothing more than a natural way of interacting socially with relatives and friends (Rakowski and Hickey, 1976). Reporting of experiences through reminiscence may be the only way an older person may feel he or she can contribute actively to a conversation. *Although older persons should be encouraged and assisted to live in the present, reminiscence serves an important function and should not be discouraged or ignored.*

Assets

We seldom consider the assets an older mind brings to a situation. For example, an older person's vocabulary tends to remain intact and may even increase during the later years (Gilbert, 1977). Also, older persons gather a great deal of general information throughout their years of experience and study (Gilbert, 1977). Often they retain much of that information, especially if they continue to read, listen to the news and to educational programs, and relate to other people on a regular basis. Verbal reasoning and judgment are also assets of growing older (Gilbert, 1977). Much of this comes from the wealth of experience an older person has obtained.

Creativity is another asset we seldom consider. Persons who are creative tend to remain creative throughout their lives (Gilbert, 1977). Some people have been too busy with other things to pursue their creativity. When they have more time, they begin developing creative pieces of work. For example, Grandma Moses did not begin painting until she was quite old.

These are only a few of the assets of growing older. There are many more, but the important thing to remember is that there are assets. *As a caregiver, it is important that you try to recognize your older family member's assets as you relate to him or her. Try to remain alert to your own assets as you grow older.* Some changes may take place in our minds as we grow older. However, if people keep their minds active, if they remain interested in people and things around them, and if they remain open to learning new things, they will likely remain more mentally alert than those people who are inactive and uninterested in the world around them (Gilbert, 1977).

Alzheimer's Disease

Some caregivers relate to an older person suffering from Alzheimer's Disease. If you are one such caregiver, you should recognize that your older family member is experiencing many changes within his or her mind. He or she may have been extremely active and interested in others and still is experiencing severe short-term memory loss; lack of judgment; confusion; changes in personality, behavior, and mood; and is not able to take care of his or her personal needs (Gwyther, 1982). This is a tragic disease that causes mental deterioration. It accounts for approximately 50%-60% of all dementing illnesses. Approximately 5% of people 65 years and older and 20% of people over 80 suffer from a dementing illness (Zarit, 1979). So far no definite cause, prevention, or cure for this disease has been found. In Chapter 4 we will discuss ways of relating to persons who have severe memory losses and dementing illnesses.

If you are caring for an older person who is experiencing symptoms of Alzheimer's Disease or another dementing illness, be sure he or she is evaluated by a physician who is familiar with the disease. It could be that he or she is not actually suffering a dementing illness but is experiencing some of these symptoms as a result of medication, poor nutrition, high blood pressure, a combination of alcohol and other drugs, or for other reasons. Often these situations can be treated so that the confusion and memory loss disappear.

WHAT CHANGES CAN WE EXPECT IN OUR EMOTIONS AS WE GROW OLDER?

Security

Emotions do not cease as we grow older. At every age we have emotional needs. These needs are really no different for older than for younger persons (Gilbert, 1977). Security is a need we have throughout our lives. We need to have adequate housing, food, clothes, love, and security in our homes (Gilbert, 1977). If an older family member is living with a caregiver's family, it is likely that he or she is receiving adequate housing, food, and clothing. He or she also needs to feel secure about being "one of the family."

Love

Closely tied to being one of the family is a need for love. Love may be especially important to an older family member if he or she has lost important things such as health, home, possessions, and perhaps, income, spouse, neighbors and/or friends (Gilbert, 1977). A caregiver can demonstrate love to an older family member by showing genuine interest, by showing affection, and by spending quality time with him or her.

Recognition and Respect

Two other needs of older people are recognition and respect (Gilbert, 1977). An older family member needs to know that he or she has worth and that the caregiver cares about his or her ideas and feelings. A caregiver should learn to recognize and respect the older person for the person he or she is now. It is important to recognize that worth is not dependent on productivity. For example, the dependent older person may not be able to fulfill his or her earlier roles of bringing home the paycheck, facilitating the family decision-making process, or volunteering for the local hospital board. But he or she may still be able to offer emotional support or provide suggestions or insights about important issues. If an older family member feels recognition and respect, he or she will likely maintain his or her self-esteem. This is also an important need. Another component for ensuring self-esteem is to allow the older dependent person to make his or her own decisions as often as possible. Also, if possible, allow the older person to be involved in family decisions.

Our physical, psychological, and emotional wellbeing are interrelated. Often a change in one affects another. The caregiver may see the interaction of these aspects when relating to the older family member. For example, if the older relative is not feeling well, he or she may become emotionally depressed. His or her depression may cause temporary memory loss. Being aware of this interaction may be helpful in understanding the reasons behind an older relative's behavior.

SUMMARY

We have covered a great deal of information in this chapter, but we have not even begun to touch on all there is to know about the physical, psychological, or emotional aspects of aging. A resources list of additional reading is provided. More detailed information is available in the following resources list. We hope that this brief overview will provide a deeper understanding of what it means to be aging.

SUGGESTIONS FOR PRACTICE

1. Set up an information seminar for family caregivers in the community. The seminar could be scheduled for three or four meetings to present information about the aging process for family caregivers. The primary objective of the seminar is educational and handouts about aging could be provided. The seminar could be advertised in the newspaper as a community service. Speakers could be invited from area agencies on aging and local colleges or universities.

2. Develop information brochures about the sensory changes individuals experience as they age. Distribute these brochures to hospitals, doctors, offices, churches, and other public locations in the community.

3. Prepare information spots about the changes older persons experience for broadcast on a local radio station. These could be presented as a public service by the radio stations.

4. Form a group of caregivers and complete the Sensory Loss Exercises. Discuss the feelings of the caregivers as they simulate some of the sensory changes experienced by older persons. How have their perceptions of their environment changed? What things can be changed in their homes to help the older persons deal with sensory changes?

SENSORY LOSS EXERCISES

It is likely that your older family member is experiencing some loss of one or more of his or her senses. The following exercises provide opportunities for you to simulate these sensory losses. You may want to select sensory losses your older family member is experiencing. Try to put yourself in your older family member's situation as much as possible.

Hearing

In order to experience hearing loss
1. Place moistened cotton balls or ear plugs in your ears and
   a. Call your friend on the telephone.
   b. Turn on the radio or TV and adjust the volume until it is comfortable for you to hear. Listen for a few minutes. Remove the cotton balls or plugs

to determine what the volume would sound like to persons without hearing impairments.
  c. With the moistened cotton balls or ear plugs in place, attend a meeting where two or more persons are likely to be speaking at one time.

Visual

In order to experience visual impairments
  1. If you wear glasses, place a plastic wrap or bag over the lens. If you do not wear glasses, wrap the plastic around goggles. This will simulate blurred vision. Now that you have blurred vision, try to
    a. read the newspaper
    b. locate the number of your doctor in the telephone book
    c. read the directions for taking a prescription drug
    d. walk through your house
  2. Instead of the clear plastic wrap, place yellow transparent film on your glasses or goggles. This simulates yellowing of the lens. Now that you have "yellowing of the lens,"
    a. attempt to differentiate colors of blue, green, and violet
    b. look in the refrigerator to see what looks good to eat
  3. Paste small spots of black paper on your goggles. This simulates spotted vision. Now that you have "spotted vision,"
    a. thread a needle
    b. sign your name on a small, thin line drawn on a paper
    c. read a newspaper

Touch

In order to experience the decreased sensation of touch
  1. Wear plastic gloves or wrap plastic around your hands. Then
    a. have someone touch or hold your hand
    b. feel objects of different texture (i.e., cotton balls, sandpaper, wood, metal)
    c. pour some tap water in a bowl and try to determine the temperature

Taste

In order to experience diminished taste
  1. Blindfold yourself and place cotton or another kind of harmless material in your nose. Then
       Try to distinguish a pear from an apple

Smell

In order to experience diminished smell
1. Place cotton or another kind of harmless material in your nose. Then
   a. Put an amount of your favorite perfume or cologne on that "smells" good to you. Take out the cotton and see how potent it is.
   b. Put on a blindfold and place cotton in your nose. Try to distinguish an onion from an apple.

Dexterity

In order to experience diminished dexterity
1. Tape pencils or pieces of sturdy cardboard to the backs of fingers. This will simulate the stiffness of arthritis. Then
   a. button your blouse or shirt
   b. pick up a coin from a countertop
   c. open a medicine bottle
   d. open a carton a of milk
   e. tie a necktie or ribbon
2. To simulute paralysis that may result from a stroke, use one hand to
   a. tie your shoe
   b. open a medicine bottle
   c. button your shirt or blouse
   d. put on slacks

Mobility and Balance

In order to experience decreased mobility and balance
1. Spin around in circles. Then attempt to walk in a straight line. This will simulate dizziness.
2. If you have access to a wheelchair, try to wheel it from one room to another with only one hand and leg.
3. If you have the use of a walker or cane,
   a. try to carry a small bag of groceries and another small package while using one of the aids
   b. pick up a book from the floor while still grasping the walker or cane
4. Put on a pair of shoes that are several sizes too large. Walk through the house with them.

RESOURCE LIST

To obtain more information about the aging process you may want to explore the following resources:

Books

Atchley, R. C. (1980). *The social forces in later life.* (3rd ed.). Belmont, CA: Wadsworth.

Butler, R. N. (1975). *Why survive? Being old in America.* New York: Harper & Row.

Cohen, S. Z., & Gans, B. M. (1978). *The other generation gap.* Chicago: Follett.

Curtin, S. R. (1972). *Nobody ever died of old age.* Boston: Little, Brown.

Ernst, M., & Shore, H. (1978). *Sensitizing people to the processes of aging: The in-service educator's guide.* Denton, TX: North Texas State University, Center for Studies in Aging.

Hickey, T., & Fatual, B. (1978). *Sensory deprivation and the elderly–Gerontology practitioner training manual.* University Park: The Gerontology Center, Pennsylvania State University.

L'Engle, M. (1979). *The summer of the great grandmother.* New York: Seabury Press.

MaClay, E. (1977. *Green winter–Celebrations of old age.* New York: McGraw-Hill.

Neuhaus, R., & Neuhaus, R. (1982). *Successful aging.* New York: John Wiley.

Ragan, P. K. (Ed.). (1979). *Aging parents.* Los Angeles: University of Southern California Press.

Rockstein, M., & Sussman, M. (1979). *Biology of aging.* Belmont, CA: Wadsworth.

Self-maintenance skills. (1976). Gerontology Practitioner Training Manuals. University Park, PA: The Gerontology Center, Pennsylvania State University.

Sine, R. D. (Ed.) (1977). *Basic rehabilitation techniques: A self-instructional guide.* Germantown, NY: Aspen.

Vining, E. G. (1978). *Being seventy–The measure of a year.* New York: Viking.

Chapter 3

STRESSFUL STRUCTURAL SITUATIONS
WITHIN THE FAMILY

Key Questions

1. What might be stressful about the ambiguous role of caregiver?
2. How might the health problems of the older family member and/or caregiver cause stress?
3. What are some of the financial difficulties experienced by many family caregivers?
4. How might the need for decision-making cause stress?
5. What might be stressful about making changes in the family routine?
6. How might role shifts cause stress for an older family member and his or her caregiver?
7. How can the caregiver divide his or her time to reduce the stress he or she feels from competing demands?

An occupational therapist, in talking about her work in home health care, said she could expect to relate to someone almost every day—either a dependent elderly person or his or her caregiver—who would cry because of the stresses accompanying his or her situation (Roll, 1981). The stresses of caregiving are tremendous. Caregivers experience them every day. In this chapter we shall be discussing some of the situations that may be causing stress, as well as some possible ways to relieve stress. As a caregiver, you may be able to relate to much of the material.

Caregiving stresses are interrelated (Schmidt, 1980). The effects of one stress may directly or indirectly influence the caregiver's functioning. For example, the added expenses of caregiving may require a woman to find employment outside of the home in addition to serving as the primary caregiver for her husband. This may lead to role overload. Role overload may cause fatigue. Fatigue may cause the woman to become impatient with her husband. Her impatience may precipitate marital conflict not experienced before in their relationship. Figure 3.1 presents the interrelationships between caregiving responsibilities and stress. *The interrelatedness of stress means that we can seldom look at each source of stress individually. In order to determine appropriate interventions, each unique situation needs to be viewed in its entirety.*

WHAT ARE SOME STRESS-PRODUCING SITUATIONS?

The Undefined Role

Today, when someone is employed, he or she can expect to have a job description to help him or her know how to carry out the tasks of the job effectively. We also have an understanding of certain expectations society has for people who are in roles such as mother, father, or grandmother. Although these expectations are not formalized in a job description, people usually know something of what others expect of them in their particular role. What is your job description or role as caregiver? There are few social guidelines for the role of caregiver to the elderly (Getzel, 1981). A caregiver may not know how much care is appropriate to give, if certain feelings are appropriate, or which of your own needs are appropriate to meet. There is no formal way to measure whether you are overdoing or underdoing your tasks. This uncertainty may be a source of stress for you (Getzel, 1981).

In addition to job descriptions, workers often have access to some type of training to prepare them for their jobs. Again, this is usually unavailable to caregivers. Caregivers are willing to give support but many times are not provided with information needed to develop caregiving skills (Silverman and Brahce, 1979). Sometimes frustration is experienced because little is known about the aging process and how to respond to an older family member. In some instances, the caregiver may be overly protective and encourage dependence rather than independence. Without information it may be difficult to know how to respond to behavioral changes in an older family member.

A caregiver may feel that he or she did not have time to prepare for the responsibilities of caring for an older family member. The need to serve as a caregiver may have come suddenly and unexpectedly (Hausman, 1979; Miller, 1981). This book, we hope, will be helpful in learning more about being a caregiver.

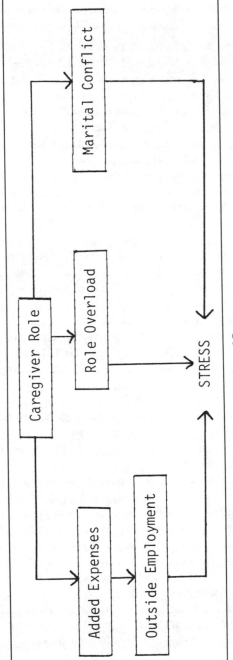

FIGURE 3.1: Interrelations Between Caregiving Responsibilities and Stress

Health

Some of the stresses a caregiver experiences may relate to his or her health condition, to the deteriorating health of a dependent family member or both. Some caregivers are older and may be suffering from a chronic illness. Others may be as disabled as the person they are caring for. These individuals have been termed the "hidden patient" by Fengler and Goodrich (1979). In a study they completed of elderly wives who were serving as caregivers, they discovered that more than half had significant illnesses of their own and were as needy as the patient. A mechanical lift may have been installed in a home because the caregiver was unable to help his or her family member move from the bed to a chair. Or perhaps a family member uses a wheelchair because the caregiver does not have the strength to help him or her walk.

Sometimes the stresses of caregiving cause increased health problems for the caregiver (Crossman et al.,1981). For example, one woman developed hypertension while serving as a caregiver and later suffered a disabling stroke. She was no longer able to care for her husband, who had also been disable by a stroke. Some caregivers have come to the point of complete exhaustion. In one study it was found that exhaustion of the caregiver was second only to unmanageability in causing the family to institutionalize their older family member (Schmidt, 1980). Adult children sometimes encourage one parent to be placed in a nursing home in order to "save" the other parent.

Health can be a problem for a caregiving child as well as spouse. With the increase of longevity, it is becoming more and more common for children around 60-70 years of age to care for parents who are 80–90 years old. The parents become dependent at a time when the children are experiencing a decline in strength and energy.

This information is not meant to frighten caregivers but to encourage them to look seriously at their situation and make any necessary adjustments to protect their own health as they serve as caregiver. A caregiver will not be able to continue as a caregiver if he or she becomes dependent. *It is important to evaluate whether keeping a family member at home is realistic.* If it is realistic, caregivers can explore what other people and services might assist them so that they can protect their own physical and emotional well-being as they continue to serve as caregivers.

Even if a caregiver is healthy, the deterioration in health of an older family member may be stressful (Johnson and Bursk, 1977). It is likely that a caregiver will experience pain as he or she watches his or her older family member suffer and become increasingly dependent. As the older family member becomes more dependent, the caregiving role becomes more strenuous (Getzel, 1981). This may increase frustration for both the caregiver and the family member and may cause new family conflicts (Johnson and Bursk, 1977). In this situation, *it is important for the caregiver to have sufficient time away from caregiving responsibilities in order to tend to his or her own needs.*

With the increase in longevity, caregivers more frequently find themselves caring for more than one older family member (Fengler and Goodrich, 1979). For example, an adult child may find herself caring for a dependent spouse as well as a dependent parent. This situation will undoubtedly increase the amount of stress with which she must cope. Again, a caregiver needs to evaluate whether it is realistic to attempt to be a caregiver to both a spouse and a parent.

Financial

Perhaps you experience stress because of financial difficulties in maintaining your elderly family member at home (Silverstone and Hyman, 1982). You may have needed to remodel you home (Blazer, 1978). Many of the needed supportive services are not reimbursed by Medicare or other assistance programs, so they need to be picked up by the family. This is especially problematic for older persons on fixed incomes. One woman expressed her need:

> The most difficult thing for me to do is pay the bills. Finding the money is difficult to cope with. . . . I took out a loan to pay the doctor bill last year. Now I owe the bank $800, and I have already overspent this year [Frankfather et al., 1981: 40].

Perhaps some caregivers have not been able to get a loan. If they have a low income, they are not able to afford services and products that might make caring for a dependent family member less stressful (Fengler and Goodrich, 1979). Others may experience stress because of competing financial needs for their inadequate resources. Should a caregiver buy his or her daughter a needed winter coat or his or her mother a needed pair of shoes?

Some may have found it necessary to seek paid employment in order to meet the added expenses of caring for an older family member. As stated in an earlier example, this can cause role overload (Fengler and Goodrich, 1979) and caregivers may feel they are doing a poor job both at work and as caregivers (McGreehan and Warburton, 1978).

Some may have felt financially secure as they began their caregiving experience. However, savings may be drained because of an increase in expenses and the long duration of caring for an elderly family member. Some may worry about what expenses will develop in future years.

Discovering financial resources to meet each of the unique situations and set of needs is a complicated task that is beyond the capacity of this chapter. Even though it may cost money a caregiver does not seem to have, he or she may find professional financial and legal advice to pay off in the long run. What we can do, however, is look in a general way at potential financial resources for a caregiver.

When considering potential sources of income to help finance the care of an older family member, the caregiver may want to ask the older person to assist with the financial burden through pensions, social security income, savings accounts, real estate, automobiles, or other potential sources of capital (Mace and Rabins, 1981). The older person's health insurance and major medical insurance may be a resource. These may help pay for home care or needed equipment. Many older family members qualify for Medicare. Check with a local Social Security Administration office to see what expenses Medicare will cover.

Medicaid, a federal program, is another potential resource. Because this program is administered by individual states, each state has its own rules and regulations about what services it covers and the eligibility requirements. Detailed information about this program can be obtained from the Department of Social Services or the Welfare Department.

Also, the caregiver or older family member may qualify for tax benefits. Contact the Internal Revenue Service or a tax consultant to explore the "breaks" for which you qualify. You may also want to explore other state, federal, and private funding sources such as food stamps or Meals-on-Wheels programs (Mace and Rabins, 1981).

Other sources to consider are other family members. They may wish to contribute financially to the expenses of an older family member. This may already be a source of stress for some caregivers, perhaps siblings or other relatives are not making equal financial contributions to meet an older family member's expenses. Or perhaps one relative is angry with another relative. Perhaps both relatives share their frustrations with the caregiver and as a result, the caregiver feels caught in the middle. If this is occurring, the caregiver may find it helpful to communicate honestly yet sensitively with both relatives. The caregiver or another relative may not be aware of the tight financial situation. An arrangement may be made with a relative to have him or her contribute time instead of money. For example, the caregiver and three siblings may have decided to hire a woman to stay with their mother four afternoons a week so the caregiver can run errands or spend time with friends. If one of the siblings is unable to pay his or her share of the expenses, perhaps the woman can be hired for three days a week and the brother or sister could "pay" his or her share by staying with the mother one afternoon a week. With his or her payment of time, the caregiver could still get away four afternoons a week. If the caregiver and other family members cannot seem to resolve the financial conflicts, it may be helpful to seek professional help. Social workers, counselors, and ministers are good sources of counsel.

Making Decisions

Needing to make decisions causes stress for caregivers. For example, who should make the decision? The dependent older person used to make it. Or when should we decide? Can we wait a little longer? Should mother move in with us? Should she move to a nursing home? She wants to live alone. Should we overrule her? What is best for Aunt Mary? Does she know or do *we* know best? Decisions! Decisions! Do you feel overwhelmed by all the decisions that need to be made when you care for a dependent older family member?

One of the most unhappy times in your life may come when a family must help make decisions concerning the possible relocation of an older family member (Brandwein and Postoff, 1980). These decisions may bring feelings of guilt and anger in both you and the older relative (McGreehan and Warburton, 1978). This stress may be lessened if the older family member, you, and any others affected by the decision can be involved in the decision-making process (Miller, 1981). However, this is not always possible. Some may have already made decisions concerning the care of an older family member without involving him or her in that decision. Perhaps the older relative was unable to be involved in the decision-making process. Or perhaps the caregiver did not realize the importance of including him or her.

Changes in Family Routine

Let us assume that a decision has been made. For our purposes, we will focus on the decision to move an older dependent family member into a caregiver's home. An additional person in the home requires changes in family routine and many other family issues (Brubaker and Brubaker, 1981).

These changes require many adaptations and, consequently, the potential for stress.

Let us look at some of the possible changes. If an extra person moves into a home, space becomes an issue (Brubaker and Brubaker, 1981; McGreehan and Warburton, 1978). If the older person moves into the caregiver's home and children are still at home, the caregiver may have asked one of the children to give up his or her room. The child may feel some resentment toward his or her grandparent because of having to give up his or her "turf." He or she may have to move in with a sibling, causing another child to feel some resentment. The older person may blame himself or herself for the disruption and feel guilty, frustrated, and/or depressed (McGreehan and Warburton, 1978). *Open and sensitive communication among family members is important in this situation and may alleviate some of the stress experienced by all. It will be helpful if each family member affected by the decision can be a part of the decision-making process.*

Even if space is not an issue, home furnishings and management may be (McGreehan and Warburton, 1978). The older relative has his or her own furnishings. How will these be incorporated into the new home? What if you and he or she have dissimilar preferences? What if you cannot tolerate his or her furnishings? It will be helpful if some of these furnishings, knick-knacks, and other memorabilia can be incorporated into the older person's new "home." This may call for some compromise on the part of other family members. The caregiver and other family members may be asked to display some things they would not choose to have in their home. However, *for the new home to really seem like home, the older person needs to have access to some of his or her meaningful surroundings.*

Management may be another issue. Who makes the decisions? Must your older relative defer to your wishes because he or she is living in your home? Again, open and sensitive communication between the older family member and the other family members is important as these decisions are made.

Another issue that calls for flexibility and adaptation is the role of the older person in his or her new surroundings. Is he or she a "guest" or an integral part of the family? Is he or she included in the family chores (chosen according to his or her capabilities) or is he or she constantly served? Is the older person free to raid the refrigerator as he or she wishes even though he or she is supposed to follow a special diet (don't other adults have choices as to whether to "cheat" on their diets)?

What about entertaining friends? The friends include the caregiver's friends, the caregiver's children's friends, and the older relative's friends.

Should the older relative always be included when the family entertains friends? What if the older relative wants to be included and you prefer that he or she is not there? Or what happens if you think it would be good for the older family member to join in the group and he or she prefers to withdraw to his or her room?

What about children's friends? Should children still be allowed to have a group of friends over for a party even if the older person becomes agitated by the noise? Can a compromise be made? Does the child feel he or she must always give up things for the older person? Incidentally, the older person may also feel badly about this.

And what about the older relative's friends? Should the caregiver be present when friends come to visit him or her, or should you make a point to be out of the room or out of the home during that time? What happens if friends of the older person drop in to visit at the same time the caregiver is entertaining friends? What happens if you do not like the older family member's friends, or vice versa?

Each family will need to find its own solutions to these situations. One way for a family to begin working at these issues is to hold a family conference (Mace and Rabins, 1981). Each person who is affected by the decisions should be present at the conference and given an opportunity to be as actively involved in the decision-making process as he or she is able. If the family decides to hold a conference, you may want to ask for the assistance of an outside person such as a minister, social worker, or counselor. An outsider will be able to listen objectively and can help focus on the appropriate issues. They may be able to share helpful insights that your family cannot perceive because you are too close to the situation to look at it objectively (Mace and Rabins, 1981).

Another issue involves leisure time and vacations. The caregiver may fear leaving the elderly family member alone while he or she is involved in a recreational activity or away on vacation. It may not be possible to leave the older family member alone. If this is the case, arrangements need to be made for a substitute caregiver any time you are away from home.

Having a dependent older adult move into your home requires that both your family and older relative give up some independence. All will need to give up some privacy, which may cause stress for everyone. It will be helpful if these issues can be anticipated and worked out before the move. All family members should be given the opportunity to state what their preferences are and to indicate what compromises they are willing to make. Even after decisions are made, it will likely be necessary to make adjustments as different problem areas surface.

These are only a few of the adjustments that need to be made as an older dependent family member leaves his or her home to move in with another family member. Many caregivers have experienced these as well as others.

Role Shifts

As a caregiver, think about either your marriage or a marriage. Who is responsible to repair a car? pay the bills? do the laundry? cook the meals? fix a leaky faucet? Would you assign some of these tasks to a wife and others to a husband? Many married couples have either formally or informally assigned certain tasks to each other (Brubaker and Hennon, 1982; Keith and Brubaker, 1979). Some tasks may be shared, but often tasks are performed primarily by either the wife or husband. If the husband or wife becomes ill and is no longer able to carry out his or her assigned responsibilities, this may upset the balance. For the first time ever, you may have to take care of the family finances or arrange for a repair to be made on your home. Or you may need to do laundry and cook the meals. You may not know where to begin. This role change may cause conflict and confusion for both you and your spouse (Crossman et al., 1981). You may be frustrated with needing to learn so many new things at a time when you already feel emotionally drained. The dependent spouse may feel frustrated and experience loss of self-esteem because he or she is no longer able to express his or her worth in the usual ways. Most likely it is more difficult for the dependent older person to relinquish his or her duties as it is to deal with the fears, lack of experience, and increased time and energy commitment involved in assuming the new roles.

Role shifts also become an issue for adult children and their dependent parent (McGreehan and Warburton, 1978; Silverstone and Hyman, 1982; Robinson and Thurner, 1979; Goodman, 1980; Miller, 1981; Hartford and Parsons, 1982). The term "filial maturity" is used to describe the role shifts between adult children and older parents. Please note that a role *shift* takes place rather than a role *reversal*. In a healthy relationship, a child does not become a parent to his parent (Blenkner, 1965)—the parent will always be the parent. However, in reaching filial maturity, the adult child no longer relates to parents as a *dependent* child but as an *adult* child. The filial role involves being depended upon (Blenkner, 1965). The child is able to accept his or her parent as human and forgive him or her for past and current conflicts. The child recognizes and responds to the parent's needs (Goodman,

1980). At the same time, the child recognizes his or her own humanness, limits, and needs.

It takes a great deal of effort, understanding, patience, trial and error, self-acceptance, and self-evaluation to reach filial maturity (Goodman, 1980). Both the child and the parent may feel tension and conflict throughout this process (McGreehan and Warburton, 1978). It may be hard to give up the belief that parents are omnipotent and immortal. Parents may deny their increasing dependence by withdrawing or by attempting to regain some control over the child in order to compensate for other losses they are experiencing. In order for filial maturity to take place, both the child and parent need to accept necessary role shifts.

Role shifts do not mean that the adult child-parent or spouse relationships can no longer be relationships of mutual support and aid (Miller, 1981). Even though a parent or spouse may need to relinquish some duties, there are other ways for them to express their worth and support. For example, a parent or spouse may still be able to give emotional support, or he or she may be able to offer advice and wisdom resulting from many years of experience and study.

The fact that you are a caregiver implies that you have needed to make a role shift with the older person for whom you are providing some care. The next issue, then, is determining the amount of responsibility you will assume. The amount of responsibility assumed for an older family member will affect how dependent or independent he or she will be. How much responsibility *should* you, as a caregiver, assume? When is it appropriate to take over the tasks performed earlier by the older family member? When is it inappropriate to assume certain tasks? A caregiver can mean well by taking over for an older family member and yet cause harm to him or her by doing so. Sometimes it is easier to do something for an older relative than watch while he or she struggles to complete the task. Sometimes it may seem as though the short time available to complete a certain task dictates that the caregiver complete it. Other times the caregiver may unknowingly behave as though the older family member is totally dependent when, in fact, he or she needs to depend on you for only one or a few things. One older woman experiencing this situation stated in frustration, "Just because I need help crossing the street doesn't mean I don't know where I'm going!" (Miller, 1981).

It is important that the caregiver encourage the older family members to be as independent as they possibly can. This may mean they assume *small* responsibilities, such as deciding which of two vegetables to eat for dinner or which pair of pajamas to wear to bed. Even if the older family member cannot cook or dress himself or herself, it is likely he or she still has preferences regarding issues of food and clothing. If the older relative does not seem to care about the decision, it is still important to encourage him or her to be involved in issues surrounding his or her care.

Sometimes the task will seem very frustrating because the older person may resist doing something you know he or she can do. At other times you will not know whether he or she can perform the task. To further complicate things, there are appropriate times and circumstances when the caregiver needs to make decisions and take responsible action for the older family member because he or she can no longer manage (Hartford and Parsons, 1982). Even though it is important to make every effort to place the mastery of an older relative's life in his or her own hands, there are times when he or she may feel deserted and will become overly anxious if he or she needs to make decisions. As a caregiver, how do you know what to do? Often you will not know for sure. You may need to make a decision based on what you think is best at that time. Later you may find something else to be better. You may find it helpful to talk with your older family member's doctor and/or social service provider to discuss the specifics of his or her situation. They can help you form a better idea of what is too much or not enough responsibility for your older family member to assume.

Has the caregiver been able to accept a different role with the dependent family member? The caregiver may resent it that a spouse, parent, or other relative has become so dependent on him or her. Caregivers may equate dependency with old age and therefore develop fears about their own aging. They may wonder if they will experience the same disability as their older family member as they grow older. To ease some of those fears, *it is important to remember that each person ages in a very unique way—no one will experience the same losses or intensity of loss.*

As you are caregiving, it is important to evaluate how you feel about your own aging. It has been suggested that the feelings people have about old age in general can greatly affect their behavior toward older persons (Silverstone and Hyman, 1982). A caregiver's feelings about his or her own aging can influence how he or she relates to the older family member.

Competing Demands

Stress may also come with the situation of competing demands. The caregiver may be caught between the demands of caring for an elderly parent and the demands of a spouse and children. Spouses and children may subtly increase their demands to counter the demands of a parent (Schmidt, 1980). Children may feel jealous of the time a caregiver spends with a parent

(Silverstone and Hyman, 1982). It may seem to them that the caregiver never does anything fun with them because he or she is always spending time with the dependent relative. Or they may feel the only way to get the caregiver's attention is to rebel or misbehave.

A spouse may also resent the amount of attention a caregiver gives to a parent. He or she may have disliked the parent throughout the marriage. His or her feelings may intensify as involvement with the parent increases. Or the spouse's relationship with his or her own family may influence how he or she responds to the older relative (Silverstone and Hyman, 1982).

Few families purposely harass their overburdened family member (Schmidt, 1980). They may not know how to express their own needs appropriately for the caregiver's time and attention. One author (Schmidt, 1980: 261) has given the following suggestions to reduce the pressure of conflicting demands:

(1) Discuss conflicts and pressures openly with parent, spouse, and children. None of them may have been aware of the pressures you feel. Your parent may reduce his or her requests and your spouse and children may offer to help you care for your parent. If they do not offer, ask them for help!
(2) Set up specific times to be with spouse and children.
(3) Spend a time with your parent (or other family member) that is least disruptive at your home.
(4) Find someone (family member, group, social worker, friend) to share your feelings with on a regular basis.

The strain of competing demands may cause marital problems (McGreehan and Warburton, 1978). In one group of caregivers, the number of arguments with their spouses increased as they became involved with their parents (Brandwein and Postoff, 1980). In addition, competition develops when the caregiver's limited time must be divided between meeting his or her personal needs and meeting the older person's needs. As a caregiver, have you ever felt that you needed to be available at all times for your older family member—that your needs should be met only if there is any time left? If you do, we would like to encourage you to reconsider. Take time off to maintain social contacts and activities. *It is important to balance the time and energy a caregiver spends providing assistance to an older family member and the time and energy spent meeting his or her own needs* (Zarit, 1979). In fact, the caregiver will give better quality care by taking care of himself or herself. As a caregiver, you need to recognize your limits. If you do not set limits, you may feel trapped and resentful. These feelings will be expressed in your caregiving. Setting some limits and scheduling specific times on which both you and your relative can count may give a sense of security to both of you and raises the quality of care (Hausman, 1979).

CONCLUSION

This has been an overview of a few of the stress-producing situations a caregiver may experience and some possible interventions. In the next chapter we will look at other stresses—those of family conflicts, coping with emotional and behavior changes, and abuse and neglect. We will also look at possible interventions to alleviate those stresses.

SUGGESTIONS FOR PRACTICE

1. Form a discussion group of caregivers and discuss the stresses they experience as a result of providing care to a family member. Encourage the participants to share ways they deal with their stresses.

2. Encourage caregivers to define precisely the expectations associated with their caregiving role. Identify the advantages and disadvantages of being a caregiver.

3. Ask caregivers to list and discuss changes in their family lives since they have become caregivers. Are the caregivers satisfied with these changes? Are there ways to minimize the impact of these changes?

4. Either in a group or individual setting, ask caregivers to complete the Caregiver's Time Use Exercise. Then discuss the differences between the amount of time they think they *should* spend and the time they *actually* spend on the various activities. What are some ways to reduce the differences between the *expected* and *actual* amount of time spent in caregiving activities?

CAREGIVER'S TIME USE EXERCISE

One of the primary causes of stress is the unrealistic view of time devoted to the caregiving role. *A caregiver needs to estimate realistically the amount of time spent in various activities.* The distribution of time will be different for each caregiver. Further, there may be a difference between expectations and actual time spent in the caregiving role. *It is important for a caregiver to examine the expected amount and actual amount of time spent in various activities.* The following is an exercise to encourage caregivers to focus on their expectations and actual time spent in various activities.

(1) Consider a typical Monday and estimate the number of hours *you think you should devote* to the following activities.

Activity	Hours Spent
(a) sleeping	_____
(b) paid employment	_____
(c) meal preparation and consumption	_____
(d) caring for spouse	_____
(e) caring for children	_____
(f) caring for older person	_____
(g) caring for self (leisure, etc.)	_____
(h) other household tasks	_____
Total hours	24

(2) Now, think about a typical Monday and record *the actual number of hours you spent* in the following activities:

Activity	Hours Spent
(a) sleeping	_____
(b) paid employment	_____
(c) meal preparation and consumption	_____
(d) caring for spouse	_____
(e) caring for children	_____
(f) caring for older person	_____
(g) caring for self (leisure, etc.)	_____
(h) other household tasks	_____
Total hours	24

(3) If your *distribution of time on other days of the week varies considerably* from a "typical" Monday, ask yourself questions 1 and 2 for each day of the week.

(4) Compare your *expected and actual distribution of time* spent in various activities. Is there a difference between expectations and actual distribution of time? Are your expectations realistic? Does this create stress for you? Are you spending too much time on one activity? Can you realistically manage your time to achieve all your goals? How can you redistribute your time? Is the caring for an older person creating too much "role overload"?

(5) If you feel role overload, why not think about the *ideal time distribution* you would develop to meet the demands you have? In a sense, dream about the way you might change the expected and actual distributions of time. Write down your "dream time distribution." Is there any change in your "dream distribution" that may be implemented in your next week's actual distribution of time? Why not try it next week? *If the change affects the time devoted to your spouse, children, or older person, it is important to discuss the change with them.* Show them this time use exercise and try to develop a agreed upon way to redistribute your time.

RESOURCE LIST

To obtain more information about potentially stress-producing situations in the caregiving role and for dealing with these stresses, you may want to explore the following resources.

Journals

Brody, E. M. (1981). "Women in the middle" and family help to older people. *The Gerontologist, 21*, 471–480.

Brubaker, T. H., & Brubaker, E. (1981). Adult child and elderly parent household: Issues in stress for theory and practice, *Alternative Lifestyles, 4*, 242–256.

Crossman, L., London, C., & Barry, C. (1981). Older women caring for disabled spouses: A model for supportive services. *The Gerontologist, 21*, 464–470.

Fengler, A. P., & Goodrich, N. (1979). Wives of elderly disabled men: The hidden patients. *The Gerontologist, 19*, 175–183.

Hartford, M. E., & Parsons, R. (1982). Groups with relatives of dependent older adults. *The Gerontologist, 22*, 394–398.

Johnson, E. S., & Bursk, B. J. (1977). Relationships between the elderly and their adult children. *The Gerontologist, 17*, 90–96.

McGreehan, D. M., & Warburton, S. W. (1978). How to help families cope with caring for elderly members. *Geriatrics* (June), 99–106.

Books

Brubaker, T. H. (ed.). (1983). *Family relationships in later life*. Beverly Hills, CA: Sage.

Burnagin, V. E., & Hirn, K. P. (1979). *Aging is a family affair*. New York: Lippincott/Crowell.

Cohen, S. Z., & Gans, B. M. (1978). *The other generation gap*. Chicago: Follett.

Frankfather, D. L., Smith, M. J., & Caro, F. G. (1981). *Family care of the elderly*. Lexington, MA: D. C. Heath.

Giles, J. (1981). *A guide to caring for and coping with aging parents*. Nashville, TN: Thomas Nelson.

Goodman, J. G. (1980). *Aging parents: Whose responsibility?* Workshop Models For Family Life Education, Family Service Association of America, 44 E. 23rd St., New York, NY 10010.

Loss reaction and grief management. (1976). Gerontology Practitioners Training Manuals. University Park: Gerontology Center, Pennsylvania State University.

Mace, N. L., & Rabins, P. V. (1981). *The 36-hour day: A family guide to caring for persons with Alzheimer's Disease, related dementing illnesses and memory loss in later life*. Baltimore: Johns Hopkins University Press.

Otten, J., & Shelly, F. (1976). *When your parents grow old*. New York: Funk and Wagnalls.

Ragan, P. K. (Ed.). (1979) *Aging parents*. Los Angeles: University of Southern California Press.

Schwartz, A. N. (1977). *Survival handbook for children of aging parents*. Chicago: Follett.

Silverstone, B., & Hyman, H. H. (1982). *You and your aging parent* (expanded ed.). New York: Pantheon.

White, D., & Neal, M. (1981). *A guidebook for the family and friends of older adults*. Portland: Institute on Aging, Portland State University.

Chapter 4

STRESSFUL EMOTIONAL SITUATIONS
WITHIN THE FAMILY

Key Questions

1. What are some of the family conflicts causing stress?
2. How might a caregiver respond to behavioral changes in his or her older family member in order to reduce stress?
3. How might a caregiver deal with mood changes experienced by his or her family member?
4. What are some of the emotional responses a caregiver might expect to receive?
5. What kinds of abuse and neglect have been found in the caregiving experience? What can be done to prevent abuse and neglect?

In this chapter we will continue our discussion of the potentially stress-producing situations in the caregiving role. We will look at family conflicts, behavioral and mood changes in the dependent person, emotional reactions of the caregiver, and abuse and neglect. We will also discuss some interventions and coping mechanisms for these situations. Caregivers are the "experts" on stressful emotional situations within the family. They are the ones who experience these situations daily and develop coping mechanisms and interventions to lessen the stress of these situations. They are the ones who can offer empathy and understanding to each other. We hope this chapter will encourage you to examine your stressful situation and consider ways to reduce the stress.

WHAT MIGHT BE SOME OTHER
STRESSFUL SITUATIONS FOR A CAREGIVER?

Family Conflicts

Every family has conflicts because family members relate so closely to one another. However, *the dynamics of the caregiving situation have the potential for deepening old or bringing about new conflicts* (Brubaker and Brubaker, 1981). These conflicts can cause stress. We cannot cover all of the potential family conflicts within the caregiving situation, but we will look at several.

It might be important for us to look first at how you were chosen to be the caregiver. In some cases the family decision as to who should become a caregiver occurs automatically. The family may just assume that a certain member will serve as a caregiver. If the dependent person's spouse is living, he or she usually becomes the caregiver. For a parent without a spouse, the caregiver often becomes the oldest child, the most responsible child, a single child, or the child who seems closest to the parent (Archbold, 1980). If the child fitting any of the above characteristics is a male, his wife (the daughter-in-law) may become the actual caregiver (Frankfather et al., 1981). Your family may just have assumed you would serve as caregiver, but you do not want the responsibility. Your feelings about this may be expressed either verbally or nonverbally to your family members, including the relative for whom you are caring. If this is your situation, it may be helpful to reevaluate this with your family. An understanding doctor, minister, social worker, nurse, or friend may be able to provide an objective viewpoint as you look at other alternatives.

Some old patterns of relating developed by the caregiver and elderly relative may cause conflict (Brubaker and Brubaker, 1981). If the caregiver has not moved beyond the dependent child role, he or she may be unable to accept a dominant parent's decline (Schmidt, 1980), or may deny that mother or father is no longer able to do something physically or ignore the confusion he or she is experiencing. If a parent's behavior can no longer be ignored, you may think your parent is intentionally behaving in that manner. As a result, impatience and anger may characterize your relationship with your parent. If you can understand that your parent is no longer able to do some things he or she once did, you may be more understanding and accepting of his or her current behavior.

These same dynamics could be true in relating to a spouse if he or she was the dominant one in the relationship. A caregiver needs to come to terms with his or her view of the spouse and adjust it to match his or her current functioning.

A potential conflict comes with the death of a favorite parent (Schmidt, 1980). You may feel obligated to care for the other parent, with whom you never got along. The surviving parent may not have met your childhood dependency needs. Because of this, you may now have difficulty in responding to your parent's dependency needs (Miller, 1981). To add to this already conflictual relationship, the dependent parent may have resented the close relationship you had with the deceased parent. He or she may now continually badger you about it.

If there are any negative feelings between the caregiver and elderly relative, it is unlikely that they can be ignored, given that both will be spending much more time together. What may have been ignored earlier through distance can no longer be ignored. It may be worthwhile to seek professional help to resolve any conflicts between the caregiver and older family member that cannot be resolved.

Some may be experiencing family conflict because of sibling rivalry (Schmidt, 1980). Those who do not have siblings may be able to relate this situation to another relative, as many times another relative takes the place of a sibling in the caregiving situation. One person who has led several groups for caregivers found that many of them felt varying degrees of resentment toward siblings (or other relatives) whom they perceived as not carrying their load of the caregiving responsibilities (Hausman, 1979). In some situations the sibling who was doing very little of the actual care seemed to be receiving much approval and warmth from the dependent parent, whereas the actual caregiver felt his or her parent's anger and lack of appreciation. One caregiver expressed her feelings: "I'm the meat and potatoes in my parents' lives, but my brother is the champagne" (Silverstone and Hyman, 1982). Some of the sibling rivalry conflicts in a current caregiving situation may be carryovers from childhood sibling rivalry (Hausman, 1979). Perhaps the same dynamics of your childhood are still at work 30, 40, or 50 years later.

A caregiver may feel overburdened because of lack of involvement from other family members. Some caregivers give other relatives the impression that they do not want help but rather want to assume full responsibility for the older relative's care. These relatives, then, may eventually stop offering to help (Silverstone and Hyman, 1982). If you, as a caregiver, feel abandoned by other family members, you may want to evaluate the cues you have been sending them about your desires for their help. For others family members do *not* get as involved as they could even though their assistance is requested. It may be that a caregiver needs to give up on them and look for other people to give assistance.

You may at times feel "under fire" from other family members. This is another potential cause of family conflict. The "fire" may come from the most unexpected person(s)—from a sibling who seems to not care about the dependent parent or from great-aunt Mary who lives 2,000 miles away. Have you ever planned something that was acceptable to your older relative, only to have an "absent" relative come on the scene to share his or her criticisms and upset your relative? The "critics" may not make real trouble, but they can be very irritating (Silverstone and Hyman, 1982). They may find comfort in criticizing in order to appease their guilt for not being more involved.

If you have both your children and a dependent relative in your home, you may experience conflict regarding child-rearing techniques (Mc-Greehan and Warburton, 1978). The older relative may insist that there is a better way to discipline the children than the way you have chosen. You may not welcome his or her advice and feel increased stress in your relationship (Brubaker and Brubaker, 1981).

Children may share caregiving responsibilities (Silverstone and Hyman, 1982). Some may enjoy the responsibilities and opportunities to relate to their older relative; others may resent the older relative because he or she causes a disruption to the household. Perhaps your son is angry that he had to move out of his room so Grandma could move in. Or, perhaps your teen-agers resent Grandpa being around because they can no longer play their radio as loudly as they would like. If you suspect that your children feel resentful of your older family member, it will be helpful for you to talk with them about their feelings.

A caregiver may feel his or her older relative is playing games, and this can be a source of conflict (Silverstone and Hyman, 1982). He or she may be manipulating or denying or exaggerating his or her dependencies and belit-tling himself or herself. The older relative's behavior may influence your behavior. *It is important to try to understand the older relative's needs that cause him or her to play games.* If the caregiver can respond to the needs rather than to the games, perhaps the games will stop. A social worker or family counselor can help you evaluate this and find new and more effective ways of responding to an older relative.

Money and other material possessions often are sources of family con-flict. If families do not openly discuss certain issues related to money, they may experience conflict. Who contributes what amount to the care of the older relative? Do family members contribute equal amounts? Should the caregiver be excused from contributing money because many other respon-sibilities fall to him or her?

Money can become a substitute for personal contact (Silverstone and Hy-man, 1982). Perhaps a sister sends money because she lives too far away to provide care but wants to help. Maybe a brother sends money because he does not want to provide care for mom and sending money relieves some of the guilt he feels. Money can have power (Silverstone and Hyman, 1982). If a brother gives his father the most money, he may feel it is his right to make decisions about him.

Families may compete for inheritances. Other family members may ac-cuse the caregiver of providing care for an older relative so he or she will inherit the most. Other family members may try to discredit the caregiver to the older relative to dissuade him or her from leaving everything to the caregiver.

Family conflicts experienced during an older person's illness or period of dependency may be so deep and painful that they never heal (Silverstone and Hyman, 1982). Relationships between certain relatives may break off com-pletely. Some relationships may have been problematic before and the care-giving situation serves "as the straw that broke the camel's back." Other conflicts can be resolved either by families alone or with the help of outsid-er's. If any caregivers are experiencing intense family conflicts—either these mentioned or others—that cannot be resolved, they may wish to con-tact a doctor, social worker, family counselor, minister, or another profes-sional to assist in reducing the tension.

The preceding has focused heavily on the negative aspects of relationship patterns established prior to the caregiving situation. *It is important to rec-ognize that what has been a good relationship between the caregiver and older family member can become an even closer one.* Healthy patterns of relating include open and honest communication and consideration of each other's needs. The patterns are likely to continue in a caregiving situation if practiced previously in the relationship.

HAS THE OLDER PERSON'S BEHAVIOR CHANGED?

Other stresses come from certain behavioral changes in an older family member. Have you noticed behavioral changes in a relative? Have you ever felt irritated by his or her repeated questions, frightened by his or her wandering, angered by his or her complaints or insults, or frustrated by not knowing how to respond to his or her depression or grief? Any of these behavioral changes may be stress-producing for both the caregiver and older relative.

Memory Loss

Memory loss may be a behavioral change experienced by an older family member. The way the caregiver feels about his or her loss may influence the older relative's response to it. The older relative may try to hide the loss (Mace and Rabins, 1981). After all, who wants to admit he or she is becoming forgetful, especially when forgetfulness is frequently related to senility? However, his or her denial may prevent the caregiver from helping. The denial may also be so successful that friends are unaware of the problem and are unable to offer support (Mace and Rabins, 1981). Even the caregiver, at times, may not be able to evaluate whether an older relative has forgotten something or is acting contrary. You may have a difficult time determining what an older relative can do for himself or herself and what needs to be done for him or her. In these situations of uncertainty, a caregiver may find it helpful to arrange for psychological testing or an occupational therapy evaluation in order to obtain a realistic measure of what can be expected of the relative (Mace and Rabins, 1981). In addition to helping you be more knowledgeable as you relate to an older relative, the professional may be able to help him or her recognize his or her memory impairment and plan strategies to facilitate continued independence.

Sometimes a person's denial of memory loss may be his or her way of coping with lessening competencies (Zarit, 1979). In this situation, harm could be brought to the older person by confronting him or her with the loss. This would force a person who already has limited capacities to deal with a highly threatening situation. It would be more helpful to provide support to the older person by allowing him or her to wait to acknowledge and respond to the memory loss when he or she is ready (Zarit, 1979). As suggested earlier, it may be helpful to obtain information from skilled professionals to understand the most helpful way to respond to an older relative regarding his or her memory loss.

Simple organizational strategies can help a person compensate for his or her memory loss (Zarit, 1979). These strategies may be as simple as making lists or keeping a calendar close by in order to make appointments. Other strategies include helping persons develop routines so they can rely on habit when memory fails. They can learn to associate one behavior with another through practicing specific sequences (Zarit, 1979). A caregiver may wish to create memory aids tailored to the needs of the older person. The most effective aids will use techniques with which the relative is already familiar and that fit naturally into his or her lifestyle. Aids that are new to the person and need to be learned are less effective as the relative's deteriorating memory lessens his or her learning ability. Table 4.1 presents examples of useful memory aids.

Memory aids will not be learned over night. A caregiver will need to practice these aids with his or her relative. And not all aids will work for each person. If after practicing an aid with a relative for some time without any progress, you may want to try something else.

Repeating Questions

Repetition of questions may result from memory loss (Zarit, 1979; Mace and Rabins, 1981). The older family member may not remember things for even brief periods and so has no idea he or she is repeating a question. At other times the repetition may be a symptom of an older person's fear and insecurity. He or she may no longer understand his or her surroundings or may be very worried about something he or she is unable to express. The repetition may be a bid for reassurance. With the interaction/history caregivers have with the older relative, they may be able to pick up on a clue from the older person's questions or actions to determine what the concern really is. Reassurance can then be provided for the underlying concern. An example from the book *The 36-Hour Day* (Mace and Rabins, 1981: 103) illustrates this:

> Mr. Rockwell's mother kept asking, "When is my mother coming for me?" When Mr. Rockwell told her that her mother had been dead for many years, she would either get upset or ask the question again in a few minutes. Mr. Rockwell realized that the question really expressed her feelings that she was lost, and began responding by saying, "I will take care of you." This calmed his mother.

At other times ignoring the repetitious questions may be the most effective way of getting your relative to stop asking it. You will likely find it useless to try to convince the person that he or she is repeating a question (Mace and Rabins, 1981). You may need to practice a trial-and-error method in order to determine which response is most helpful to your family member. It is likely that one method will be best at one time and another method at another time.

TABLE 4.1
Examples of Memory Aids

I. Forgets Daily Activities

1. Make a checklist of things to do each day. If any things are to be done at a certain time, note this on the list. Write the list in large, easily read print and place it where it is seen often throughout the day.

2. Set an alarm clock for the times specific things need to be done (e.g., times for taking medication). Place a note by the alarm clock telling what is to be done at what specific time.

3. Ask a friend to call at designated times to remind you of something that needs to be done.

4. If possible, schedule important activities into well-established habits. For example, if you are to take medication in the morning and you usually use the same pan to cook hot cereal for breakfast, have someone place the medication in or near the pan before you cook breakfast.

II. Forgets Where He or She is

1. Frequently orient the person to his or her location.

2. Place several of the person's significant possessions where he or she can have easy access to them.

3. Place words or pictures on things to remind the person of their use or significance. For example, place pictures of food on the refrigerator; write "bathroom" on a sign and place it on the bathroom door.

4. If taking the person from his or her home for an appointment or visit, explain where and why he or she is going.

III. Forgets Address and Location of House

1. Buy a bracelet or necklace with the person's name and address on it.

2. Alert neighbors to the person's potential need for assistance in finding his or her home.

3. If the person can read and understand directions, have him or her place a card in a wallet or purse on which general directions are written.

4. On a card write directions for someone who finds your older family member. The card should give directions on how to locate a responsible person that your family member knows. The card should be placed where it can be found easily (i.e., taped inside the person's hat or jacket).

IV. Forgets Where Things Are Placed

1. Make a list of major items in each cupboard and drawer. Tape each list on the appropriate place.

2. Familiarize a friend or other family member with the home. Ask them for assistance if something appears to be misplaced.

3. If the older person is frequently losing his or her glasses, buy a chain to which the glasses can be attached and hang it around the older person's neck.

(continued)

TABLE 4.1 Continued

V. General Memory Aids

  1. Always have some paper and a pen available to write reminder notes. Put the notes in the same place so they can be located out of habit.

  2. Simplify the scheduling of activities. Do only things that really need to be done..

  3. Place an easily read list of important telephone numbers next to the telephone. Place the numbers in the order of the numbers used the most often to those used the least often.

  4. Have the doctor write down instructions for taking medications and other health-related suggestions.

  5. Make a list of things the older person needs to do before leaving the house (e.g., put keys in pocket or purse, make sure the stove is turned off, or lock the door).

  6. If the older person needs to learn new information, try to present the new information in small pieces at any one time.

Repeating Actions

The older person may seem to "get stuck" on one activity (Mace and Rabins, 1981), which can arouse frustration or anger in the caregiver. Sometimes gently suggesting a specific new task for the older person to do will help him or her move beyond the repetitious action. At other times, ignoring the behavior will help. As with the problem of repeating questions, a caregiver will only cause additional frustration if he or she tries to reason with the older person about stopping the behavior. Mrs. Andrews's situation illustrates this well (Mace and Rabins, 1981: 104):

> Mrs. Andrews had trouble with baths. She would wash just one side of her face. "Wash the other side," her daughter would say, but she kept on washing the same spot. Mrs. Andrews's daughter found out that gently patting her mother's cheek where she wanted her to wash next would get her out of the repetitious pattern. A stroke had lessened her mother's awareness of one side of her body. Touch is a very good way to get a message to the brain when words fail.

Wandering

Wandering is a common and often serious problem of older persons experiencing brain impairments (Mace and Rabins, 1981). A wandering older relative may present one of the most difficult problems to face for the care-giver. It appears that brain-impaired persons wander for different reasons (Mace and Rabins, 1981). It is important to understand the cause of the person's wandering behavior in order to plan ways to manage it. Mace and Rabins (1981) made the following suggestions to deal with wandering:

(1) Write simple instructions (telephone number and address) on a card to help an older person help himself or herself.
(2) Give the older person a bracelet or necklace with his or her telephone and address on it.
(3) If a move is planned, discuss the new location with the older person *before* the move.
(4) Reassure the older relative that he or she does not need to wander.
(5) The older relative's mobility may need to be restricted for his or her safety.

Clinging

An older relative's clinging behavior may cause stress. As a caregiver, have you ever felt you would go crazy because it seemed every time you turned around your older relative was there? This may be especially true for persons who are forgetful (Mace and Rabins, 1981). If this happens, it is understandable that a caregiver might feel angry, frustrated, or irritated. It may be helpful to understand some of the "whys" behind this behavior, al-though these understandings may not completely alleviate your feelings. Take a minute to imagine what the world would seem like if you constantly forgot everything you ever knew or were told (Mace and Rabins, 1981). How would *you* attempt to compensate for all the uncertainties and insecurities that must accompany forgetfulness? Wouldn't you try to stay close to some-one who offers you security?

As your older relative's caregiver, you may provide the only security he or she can remember (Mace and Rabins, 1981). It is understandable, then, that he or she would want to remain close to you. Your relative might not remem-ber that when you leave the room to go to the bathroom, change your clothes, or do something else that you will come back, so he or she may follow you.

A caregiver *does* need time alone and privacy. You may find it helpful to remind the person when you are leaving the room that you will be back. If you are sure no harm will come to your relative while he or she is alone, you may want to lock the bathroom or bedroom door when you are changing clothes. It is also important to have times when you can completely relax and be free of the caregiving responsibilities. You may want to have a friend come over to visit with your relative while you spend time by yourself, either at home or away from home (Mace and Rabins, 1981).

More behavioral problems with a relative may be noticed in the evening. It may be that the older relative's tolerance for stress is less because of having to deal with confusing perceptions all day. The caregiver's tolerance may also be less. Perhaps the older person experiences sensory deprivation in the evening because of less light. A well-lighted house may help. Or the older person may feel more confusion with the change of activity that comes in the evening. In the evening more people may be around the house, causing more noise and/or activity (Mace and Rabins, 1981). If this is possible, it may be helpful to reduce the number of things going on around an older relative in the evening. Reduce an older relative's involvement in things that may be problematic for him or her at any time of the day. Involve him or her in things that seem to be relaxing and enjoyable (Mace and Rabins, 1981). For example, if an older relative resists taking a bath, it is especially important not to attempt to make him or her take a bath in the evening. If he or she enjoys being read to or given a backrub, plan time for these activities in the evening to help relax your older relative. You may want to reduce the *number* of activities each evening (Mace and Rabins, 1981).

As a family responds to an older relative's behavioral changes, it is important to develop ways to maximize the abilities of your relative (Zarit, 1979). Take advantage of an older relative's "good" times. By interacting with him or her at these times, the caregiver and older relative may experience some mutually satisfying experiences in their relationship (Zarit, 1979). It is also important for your family to realize that even though your older relative may be impaired in some ways, he or she is not impaired in all aspects of functioning. There may be many activities he or she can enjoy with other family members. It is important to sort out what an older relative can and cannot do so that he or she is allowed to do what is possible and is not forced to attempt things he or she is unable to do.

DOES YOUR OLDER RELATIVE HAVE MOOD CHANGES?

In addition to behavioral changes, an older relative may have mood changes. All of us experience changes in mood depending on what is happening in our lives. Many circumstances demand adjustment for an older relative. It is not surprising that these may be reflected in mood changes. It is helpful to look briefly at some of these changes. For a more complete discussion, refer to Mace and Rabins (1981).

Denial

In order to cope with his or her diminishing capacities, an older relative may deny the changes he or she is experiencing. If used in moderation, denial may be a necessary mechanism for maintaining some stability (Silverstone and Hyman, 1982). However, if denial is used to the point of preventing sound decisions that may ensure the older person's safety, you or another person may need to intervene. If you are currently facing this situation, talk with your older relative's doctor or social worker about helpful ways to respond.

Hypochondriasis

The opposite reaction to denial is hypochondriasis. In this situation a person becomes obsessed with his or her health and constantly complains about physical problems that seem nonexistent (Silverstone and Hyman, 1982). This may be a way for a person to legitimately ask for attention if he or she feels left out. If you as caregiver experience this with your relative, evaluate the current pattern of relating to him or her. Do you think he or she might really be asking for something else? You may be giving him or her all the attention you feel you humanly can. Are there ways you can make the attention you give more meaningful to your older relative? Or are there ways you can expand the time he or she is interacting with others, thus relieving the burden you may feel in providing constant attention? As you evaluate your current relationship with your relative, it is also helpful to evaluate his or her past history of relating. It may be that he or she has always been somewhat hypochondriacal (Silverstone and Hyman, 1982).

Grief

It seems understandable that an older relative may be experiencing a great deal of grief. He or she may be faced with numerous losses: loss of relationships (spouse, friends, brothers and sisters), loss of material possessions (house, furnishings, car, income), loss of health to the point of needing to be taken care of, loss of independence and privacy, and loss of mastery over his or her life.

Expressions of grief can include anxiety, depression, fear, anger, and guilt (Silverstone and Hyman, 1982). These emotions are normal for persons suffering a severe loss. It is importnat for persons who are grieving to feel "OK" about expressing these emotions. It will be helpful for them to talk about their loss and express what that loss means to them. The older person's emotional well-being will be jeopardized if the person is encouraged not to grieve (Silverstone and Hyman, 1982). However, being with a person while he or she is grieving is difficult and may cause additional stress on those who may also be grieving. In situations where a caregiver feels uncertain about helpful ways to respond to an older relative as he or she is grieving, or if you feel the grieving process has continued to an unhealthy degree, you will want to seek help from a professional.

Other Mood Changes

You may find that your older relative is experiencing other mood changes, such as expressing suicidal thoughts, abusing alcohol or drugs, appearing apathetic and listless, or expressing paranoid accusations. If you notice these changes, talk with a professional about what kind of assistance may be available for your relative.

HOW MIGHT CAREGIVING AFFECT YOU?

We have talked about some of the emotions an older relative may feel. In addition to needing to respond to his or her feelings, a caregiver has his or her own emotional reactions. Although this chapter focuses on problematic areas in an attempt to find some relief as a caregiver faces those problems, it is important to acknowledge that many of the emotions you experience as a caregiver may be positive. You likely experience laughter and happiness, and feel joy, warmth, closeness, and love toward your older relative. You may find it helpful to focus on the ways you and he or she may share expressions of joy and affection (Mace and Rabins, 1981). Let's not lose sight of these positive emotions as we also look at some of the more painful emotions.

Fear of the Unknown

A caregiver should recognize that other feelings are not filled with happiness but with pain. It is natural for you to experience fear of the unknown.

You likely wonder: Will my family member get worse? Will he or she experience a brain impairment? What will happen if I can no longer care for him or her?

Loss of Freedom

You may also feel a loss of freedom. Just at the time you were ready for some relaxation and self-indulgence, you may have found yourself unexpectedly tied down and feeling trapped (Miller, 1981; Brandwein and Postoff, 1980).

Isolation

You may find yourself feeling isolated and alone (Crossman et al., 1981). Perhaps you are spending more and more time at home. This increased time at home along with increased caregiving responsibilities may mean you have less time to spend with your friends and other family members (Fengler and Goodrich, 1979). You may no longer be able to join your friends for a weekly lunch or game of golf. You may begin to feel like a prisoner in your own home (Crossman et al., 1981).

Guilt

It is common for caregivers (and other fmaily members) to feel guilty during their caregiving experience (Mace and Rabins, 1981). You may feel guilty for things you have or have not done (Silverstone and Hyman, 1982). You may feel guilty for how you treated your relative in the past—for being embarrassed by his or her behavior, for not responding to him or her in the way you really wanted to, for acknowledging that you do not really like him or her, for admitting you feel very angry about his or her dependence upon you, for wondering how long you can keep him or her at home, for wondering if it would not have been better if he or she would have died from the stroke, for wanting to spend more time with your friends and/or other family members, for being angry when you have to get out of bed night after night (Mace and Rabins, 1981)—the list could go on and on. Sometimes feelings of guilt can cause a person to feel stuck and keep him or her from making future responsible decisions that reflect the best interests of both the caregiver and the older relative. If you recognize that you are stuck because of guilt feelings, you may find it helpful to talk with an understanding minister, counselor, family member, or another caregiver. Talking with someone may help you move on and can help you place your guilt feelings in proper perspective (Mace and Rabins, 1981).

Grief

A caregiver may be experiencing his or her own grief as he or she relates to an older family member. If your spouse is experiencing a brain impairment, you may have lost him or her as your confidant (Crossman et al., 1981). This may be especially stressful because your family and friends may not recognize or understand your need to grieve this loss, and therefore not offer you the comfort they would if your spouse had died.

Adult children may also experience grief because of the change in relationship with their dependent parent. There is sadness and grief involved in remembering a parent in his or her younger years as compared to his or her current state of dependency (Brandwein and Postoff, 1980). The grief that accompanies a chronic illness may be more devastating than grief accompanying a death. The grief accompanying a caregiving role may seem to go on and on. Just when you think you have adjusted, your family member's condition may change, starting the grief process all over again (Mace and Rabins, 1981).

You may be grieving for your parent who died, just as the parent you are caring for is grieving. You may be experiencing anticipatory grief as you think about your parent's or spouse's inevitable death. Not only do you need to deal with his or her upcoming death, but you also need to watch him or her suffer throughout the illness (Mace and Rabins, 1981). Some caregivers may be grieving for a dependent parent who has already died. You may still be working through feelings related to your involvement as a caregiver. Those feelings do not automatically end with the death of your family member.

Although there are no quick and easy remedies for grief, a caregiver may find it helpful to share his or her feelings with other persons experiencing a similar situation. This may give strength to continue caring for your ill relative and/or work through some of the feelings you are experiencing as a result of your parent's or spouse's death (Mace and Rabins, 1981).

Abuse and Neglect

Many situations cause stress. A sad discovery is that in some situations stress can lead to the abuse and neglect of the person needing care (Steinmetz and Amsden, 1983; Hickey and Douglas, 1981; Chen et al., 1981). Two types of neglect have been found: passive neglect, where the elderly person is left alone, isolated, or forgotten; and active neglect, where such things as food, medicine, companionship, and bathroom assistance are withheld. Abusive treatment has included verbal and emotional abuse.

This kind of care is certainly not the norm. Many caregivers who have been abusive and neglectful have not wanted to be (Atchley and Miller, 1980: 380). They know of no other way to cope with their situation. In some instances they may have reached their limit and in a moment of frustration or rage shouted at or struck their older family member. These caregivers are not bad people. They are people who need support from others and community services to help alleviate some of their stresses.

CONCLUSION

We have discussed many stress-producing situations throughout this chapter. The stresses may seem especially profound to a caregiver who feels there is no relief in sight. In the long-term care of a dependent older adult, the burden of care may seem to weigh forever. And it appears that each of us has a limit to the amount of continuous care and support we can give others (Frankfather et al., 1981). *A caregiver needs to find and accept his or her limit.* A person is not bad if he or she cannot offer care to an older relative for as long as someone else can care for his or her relative. Neither are you better if you can care for your relative longer than someone else. All situations are different.

A caregiver needs to find ways to support and care for himself or herself while assuming the caregiving responsibilities. This support should include emotional, physical, and material support. They might receive this support from family, friends, neighbors, churches, and community service agencies. In the chapters ahead we will be looking at ways these different groups might be able to offer support. You will have the opportunity to determine the specific persons and services you think could best support you and your older family member.

CAREGIVER'S EXPECTATIONS FOR
CAREGIVING ROLE EXERCISE

Perhaps some of the stresses caregivers feel result from not knowing how much they can humanly expect to give to their older family members. They may feel they need to be available at all times and at all costs. Perhaps they have not been given permission to consider their own needs. They might not have thought about the amount of care that is reasonable for them to give. *As a caregiver, what do you expect for the caregiving role?* The following questions may help a caregiver examine his or her expectations for the caregiving role.

(1) What does your older family member *expect from you* as his or her caregiver?
    (a) amount of time per day?
    (b) amount of conversation?
    (c) amount of physical maintenance (bathing, feeding, etc.)?
    (d) amount of driving around?
    (e) other?
(2) What can your older family member *reasonably expect from you* as a caregiver? (To answer, consider the same categories listed for question 1).
(3) As a caregiver, what do you *expect from your older family member?*
    (a) understanding your work load?
    (b) assistance with household tasks?
    (c) emotional support?
    (d) financial support?
    (e) advice?
    (f) other?
(4) As a caregiver, what can you *reasonably expect from your older family member?* (To answer, consider the same categories listed for question 3).
(5) (a) What are *your older person's five most basic needs?*
    (b) Who is *responsible* to meet these needs?
(6) (a) *As a caregiver, what are your five most basic needs?*
    (b) Who is *responsible* to meet these needs?
(7) How does the caregiving role *interfere* with having your (the caregiver's) needs met?
(8) What alternatives do you have?
(9) What stresses do you and your older family member experience as a result of incongruent expectations?
(10) As a caregiver, how do you *respond* to these stresses?

SUGGESTIONS FOR PRACTICE

1. Form a group of family caregivers and discuss the conflicts they experience because they are providing care to an older family member. Which

family members feel the most stress? How can other family members help to reduce the stress? It might be helpful to have the family members share ways they have successfully reduced stress within their families.

2. Present a seminar on coping with stress. Caregivers need to examine various strategies for dealing with stress. Outline the advantages and disadvantages of each strategy. It might be helpful to present case examples of other caregiving families.

3. Develop a support group for caregivers in which they feel comfortable sharing their feelings about the caregiving situation. Encourage discussion of the participants' emotions related to their dependent older persons and the caregiving role. To provide emotional support over time, it would be beneficial if this group met regularly. Eventually, the group might evolve into a strong support group for caregivers within the community.

4. Encourage the caregivers to examine their expectations for themselves and other family members. Completion of the Caregiver's Expectations for Caregiving Role Exercise might be helpful. Are the caregiver's expectations realistic? Can they actually do what they think they should do? Can others provide as much assistance as they think they should provide? Discuss ways to develop realistic expectations for self and others.

Chapter 5

GENERAL COMMUNICATION SKILLS

Key Questions
1. What is verbal and nonverbal communication?
2. Why is communication important?
3. What are some barriers to good communication?
4. What kinds of responses facilitate constructive communication?

A baby cries. A toddler raises his arms in hopes of being held by his mother. Two teenagers discuss their exam grades. A father takes his daughter to a restaurant for lunch. A grandmother teaches her grandson to bake his favorite sugar cookies. These persons have something in common: They are all communicating.

Anyone who is alive communicates. Our daily lives include one communication experience after another. This communication takes different forms, including verbal and nonverbal cues. Even silence is a form of communication (Herr and Weakland, 1979). Through communication we share information, ideas, and meanings, influence each other, reach some understanding of each other, build trust, develop a like or dislike for persons, and learn more about ourselves and how people perceive us (Johnson, 1972; Greenberg et al., 1976).

It is common for us to take communication for granted because it is continually present in our lives. It is important for us to be aware of how we communicate. Because each communication affects our relationship with another person, it may either move the relationship forward, backward, or keep it the same (Johnson, 1972).

As someone assumes the caregiving role, he or she has the opportunity to communicate with a variety of persons—the older person for whom you are providing care, other family members, friends, neighbors, and perhaps service providers (such as doctors, lawyers, social workers). Communications with these persons may enhance or diminish the caregiver's feelings of well-being. This is not to imply that the responsibility to promote healthy communication is solely the caregiver's. Ideally, all persons should assume this responsibility. Although one cannot make others communicate responsibly, one can learn helpful ways of communicating with others. The effect of this may be more meaningful interaction. In this chapter, we discuss how to communicate more effectively with those around us. As we do this, we want to consider the needs of both the caregiver and the older person. We will look briefly at verbal and nonverbal forms of communication, barriers to communication, and responses to promote good communication.

WHAT IS COMMUNICATION?

Communication is an active process (Brill, 1973). It involves an exchange of symbols and signs between the persons involved (Greenberg et al., 1976). Some of the signs and symbols we use are verbal, the most noticeable. Other signs and symbols we use are nonverbal. A person may choose not to communicate verbally. However, it is impossible to prevent nonverbal communication (Greenberg et al., 1976). For example, a man may be very worried about something, yet not want to worry his spouse about his concern. He decides to keep his concern to himself. However, his wife may notice that something is wrong because of his pensive moods, restless nights, and poor appetite.

We express most of our communications nonverbally (Johnson, 1972). We use it more often to communicate our feelings and preferences. Our nonverbal cues may either confirm or contradict the things we communicate verbally. These nonverbal cues include the way we look, dress, and smell; our posture; how loudly or softly we speak; how fast or slowly we speak; whether we are smiling, frowning, or expressionless; whether we have eye contact with the person we talk to; our gestures; the way in which we touch or do not touch people; and the distance we maintain from others (Brill, 1973; Greenberg et al., 1976; Johnson, 1972).

Nonverbal communication is a very important component of any relationship and may convey meaning more powerfully than verbal communication (Combs et al., 1971). Table 5.1 outlines categories of nonverbal communication. As a caregiver, you may convey to an older family member feelings of closeness or distance, warmth or coldness, and approval or disapproval without saying one word (Sedgwick, 1981). Table 5.2 presents a list of nonverbal cues which are supportive and nonsupportive types of communication.

TABLE 5.1
Categories of Nonverbal Communication

1. Personal Appearance (physique, posture, body odor, dress)

Extremes in appearance or dress say something about a person—the impression he or she wishes to give and his or her feeling about himself or herself.

Posture may tell how interested the listener is. Leaning forward in a relaxed manner will encourage a person to continue talking. Not facing the person or slouching will communicate disinterest. If the speaker sits rigidly in his or her chair, this may be an indication of nervousness.

2. Tone and Volume of Voice

The meaning of words varies greatly depending on the tone and volume of voice used—whether the person is speaking in a loud or sarcastic tone or if his or her voice is very quiet and serious, for example.

3. Continuities in Speech (rate, duration, pauses)

A person communicates something more than the words spoken if he or she begins to speak in a different communication pattern than usual (e.g. beginning to speak excitedly and rapidly when his or her usual pattern is to speak calmly and slowly).

Excessively rapid speech is common when persons are experiencing anxiety.

Hesitancy in speech may indicate uncertainty or lack of confidence.

4. Eye Contact and Facial Expressions

Persons are rarely expressionless. We smile, frown, have a twinkle in our eye, show worry lines in our forehead. We often make these expressions unconsciously. Facial expressions can show apprehension, happiness, anger, passivity, friendliness, and aggression.

The amount of eye contact a person has with another communicates something to the other person. Our eyes can show that we are very interested in communication with the other person or that we are very uneasy being with him or her.

5. Gestures and Movements

These may include relaxation or tension of the body, restless movement, biting nails, shifting the feet, wringing hands, playing with a pencil, pointing, or signaling for attention. Gestures are often used to further emphasize a verbal message.

6. Touch

This is an important part of a close relationship. We all need human contact, but as we relate to people it is important for us to be aware of how they feel about being touched. Touch can show an offering of support to another person. It can also be destructive, as in battering.

7. Spatial Distance (personal space)

We each determine a "safe" distance from others when we are speaking to them. Although we need to respect each other's space, we should also be aware that being too distant may discourage communication, whereas being too close may be considered an invasion of one's privacy. This may depend on the closeness of relationship felt by the persons who are communicating.

(continued)

TABLE 5.1 Continued

8. Silence

This can be a powerful use of nonverbal communication and can express many different things. Among its meanings can be a companionable sharing, expressions of anger or despair, or recognition that a disagreement cannot be settled.

Adapted from Brill (1973), Eriksen (1979), Greenberg et al. (1976), Johnson (1972), and Zarit (1980).

WHY IS COMMUNICATION IMPORTANT?

Both verbal and nonverbal communication are extremely important to all persons. We use communication to maintain our personal stability (Bettinghaus and Bettinghaus, 1976). When we are happy, we may seek others to share our happiness. When we are discouraged, we may seek others to encourage us. When we need reassurance about a decision we make, we may talk to another person about it. When we need information, we find a newspaper, book, radio, television, or someone to whom to talk. If our normal patterns of communication are seriously disrupted, our stability is likely to become disturbed (Bettinghaus and Bettinghaus, 1976).

A person becomes more and more inactive as he or she loses opportunities to communicate (Woelfel, 1976). This inactivity promotes poor health and may even speed the aging process. If a caregiver or older family member do not have many opportunities to communicate with others, he or she may become isolated and withdrawn. This may affect physical and emotional well-being. Both may age more rapidly. The older family member may give up hope and lose interest in living. *Opportunities for positive communication experiences are important.*

WHAT MAY KEEP YOU FROM
GOOD COMMUNICATION EXPERIENCES?

Perhaps the unavailability of others with whom to communicate is one of the greatest barriers to good communication for you and your older family member. A caregiver may have noticed a decrease in opportunities to com-

TABLE 5.2
Supportive and Nonsupportive Nonverbal Communication

Nonverbal Cue	Supportive	Nonsupportive
Touching	occasional touching softly touching gentle pats	no touching sharp, abrupt touching

Eye contact	maintains good contact
	looks directly into
	    other's eye
		does not look into
		    other's eyes
		looks out the window
		    often
		closes eyes
		frequently looking
		    at watch

Gestures	head nodding when
	    appropriate
	friendly gestures
	occasional hand movements
		hand movements that
		    distract
		pointing to irrelevant
		    objects
		shaking pointed fingers

Posture	relaxed, caring posture leaning toward other	tense, rigid posture leaning away from other

Distance	close proximity to other	sitting or standing
		    away from other
		sitting or standing
		    far apart from other

Expressions	frequently smiling animated facial responses interested expressions	frowning straight faced scowling yawning

Voice volume and tone	tone and volume similar
	    to other
	soft and caring
		yelling
		talking too loudly
		talking too fast or
		    slow
		unpleasant tone

Adapted from Okun (1980), Johnson (1972), and Evans et al. (1979).

municate with others since assuming caregiving responsibilities. He or she may find himself or herself more and more isolated from other family members and friends. This isolation is likely to add to feelings of stress and frustration. If a caregiver is in this situation, it is important to seek opportunities to renew diminished contacts or develop new ones.

Similarly, an older family member needs continued opportunities for communication. A caregiver cannot and should not expect to serve as his or her only "listener." He or she needs interaction with others, including other relatives, old and new friends, and neighbors.

Another common barrier to communication is a misunderstanding between the people communicating with each other. Have you ever been surprised by a family member's or neighbor's angry response when your comment was intended as a compliment? Or have you meant something to be taken very seriously, only to find that a family member or friend completely ignored it? In these situations, the person you were communicating with understood the meaning of the message in a manner differently from that intended (Johnson, 1972). There may be several reasons for this misunderstanding.

Perhaps the person to whom you were talking did not listen carefully. Being a good listener is a difficult task and one that requires a great deal of effort. Rarely do misunderstandings come from the words we select or the way in which we organize our words; they are often caused by emotional or social reasons (Johnson, 1972). The person with whom you are communicating may have been so excited about what he or she wanted to tell you that he or she did not hear everything you said. Or it may be that the person was so sure he or she knew what you were going to say that he or she distorted what you really said to match his or her expectations (Johnson, 1972).

The way in which persons who are communicating view each other may affect their listening skills. For example, if your brother mistrusts you, he may be suspicious of what you communicate. You may pick up on this suspicion through his nonverbal cues and limit the amount of information you are willing to share with him. This may also happen with the older person for whom you are caring. You may think to yourself, "I wonder if Mom is just confused or if it really happened." Mom may pick up on your feelings of uncertainty and think, "What's the use of telling her these things? She never believes me anyway!"

Other reasons for "lost" messages include the following:

(a) The listener may feel threatened by what is being communicated. Instead of listening to what is being said, he or she may be planning a counterargument (Herr and Weakland, 1979). For example, a service provider with whom you are relating may feel threatened by the suggestions you have offered for improving your relationship. Rather than responding to your suggestions, he or she may defend his or her earlier actions.

(b) The listener may base what is being said on his or her own experiences rather than trying to "walk in the shoes" of the speaker. He or she is communicating through assumptions rather than facts (Herr and Weakland, 1979). For example, your friend may not understand how much time it takes you to find someone to stay with your relative so you can get away from home. She may become irritated with you and exclaim, "I think you just don't want to be my friend anymore!" when you are unable to just pick up and go as you did before your older relative moved in with you.

(c) The listener may be distracted by background noise or activities. It is important to provide an appropriate physical setting for the kind of communication you wish to take place (e.g., privacy for personal conversations, no background noise when communicating with the hearing impaired; Herr and Weakland, 1979). Your older relative likely will not want to discuss a sensitive issue with you if someone else is in the room. He or she also may be unable to hear your call, "Come for dinner!" if you are speaking from another room.

(d) The listener may be impatient with the person with whom he or she is communicating. Communication takes time, especially with persons whose physical and mental capacities may have diminished (Combs et al., 1971). Your father may take what seems like forever to explain things to you. You may feel you do not have the time to listen to all he has to say and so try to save time by filling in words for him and acting on your assumptions of what he wants. You may twist the conversation into a completely new direction and respond to something your father does not care about while remaining unaware of what his true needs are.

(e) The listener may not be ready to comprehend the information given to him or her (Combs et al., 1971). Perhaps your father is not emotionally ready to understand his spouse (your mother) can no longer perform housekeeping tasks. He may respond in anger, rather than in his usual understanding manner, when she asks him to vacuum the carpet.

(f) The information being given to the listener may be too late. Perhaps the listener needed the information long ago and now ignores it because of its seeming inappropriateness for this point in time (Combs et al., 1971). Your sister may try to explain for the first time her reasons for not helping you care for your mother the last six years. It may be difficult for you to hear what she is saying, her explanation being six years too late.

Further causes of miscommunication are contradictory nonverbal and verbal messages (Johnson, 1972). Sometimes we say one thing but our nonverbal cues say something very different. Does Mom believe our words that we are happy to spend time visiting with her, or does she respond to the nonverbal cues of our frequently looking at our watch and sighing? She will be confused by others' double messages. In the same way, we will be confused by others' double messages to us. Some psychologists believe that receiving contradictory verbal and nonverbal messages for an extended period of time from someone you love can result in mental illness (Johnson, 1972).

It is important for us to take note of whether our nonverbal and verbal messages are congruent. If they are not, we will need to evaluate why they are not. Perhaps we are failing to respond to our own needs verbally and our nonverbal cues show more accurately what our true feelings and needs are.

If you feel you are receiving inconsistent verbal and nonverbal messages from someone else, you may want to share your confusion with that person in an understanding and nonthreatening manner. The person may be unaware that his or her verbal and nonverbal messages are contradictory or that he or she may be too uncomfortable to express the feelings verbally.

The way in which persons express and respond to feelings may also cause miscommunication. Someone might find it difficult to deal with negative feelings—his or her own or those of others—and therefore may deny or ignore them. For example, if you express discouragement or depression to someone, he or she might say to you, "Don't feel that way." "Don't let it get you down." "Cheer up." "Things have to get better" (Johnson, 1972). Or to a person feeling a lot of pain, we might say, "Don't cry; try to think of something pleasant" (Johnson, 1972: 88). If you express anger to someone about something that happened, he or she might say, "Calm down. What good will getting angry do?" (Johnson, 1972). A more helpful response in all of these situations is to recognize the person's feelings. For example, rather than saying, "Don't cry" you might say, "Thinking about your stroke seems to make you feel sad and discouraged." Do not ask persons to deny or repress their feelings.

There seem to be several reasons why people find it difficult to express feelings. The closer feelings are to us personally, the more difficult they are to discuss openly (Johnson, 1972). If we share our feelings, we risk being rejected by the other person. In addition, many persons do not recognize many of their own feelings.

Sometimes we think it would be better to ignore our negative feelings than it would be to hurt the person toward whom we feel some negative feelings. However, our feelings are likely to be expressed one way or another. Rather than actually ignoring these feelings, we express them unconstructively. We may hurt the person more by expressing our feelings indirectly than by sharing openly how we feel about something.

If we are unaware or unaccepting of our feelings or unskillful in expressing them, we may express them unconstructively through (Johnson, 1972)

(1) labeling others ("He's really out of it.")
(2) commands ("Shut up!")
(3) questions ("Do you think it is safe to walk outside alone?")
(4) accusations ("You don't like me.")

(5) name-calling ("You're a tightwad.")
(6) sarcasm ("You certainly make a person feel wanted.")
(7) expressions of disapproval ("You're mean.")

Some of the illustrations we have presented exemplify another barrier to good communication: evaluative responses. We have a natural tendency to approve or disapprove most messages we receive from others. This happens most often when our feelings are deeply involved in the issue we are discussing. Evaluative responses often cause the other person to feel defensive and threatened (Johnson, 1972). His or her responses may be filled with evaluation and counterthreats. This complicates the communication process even further. For example, if an older family member complained that you did a poor job of combing her hair, your tendency may be to respond with a counterattack such as "At least it looks better than when you try to comb it!" If you understand that the relative's comments come from her frustration in no longer being able to comb her own hair rather than a true evaluation of how her hair looks, you may be able to respond to her in a more helpful and loving manner. It is important to try to respond with understanding rather than evaluative responses (Johnson, 1972).

If we recognize that our communication has failed with another person, we frequently blame the other person (Combs et al., 1971). It is important to remember that communication is always an interaction and the responsibility for its breakdown often lies with both participants (Combs et al., 1971).

When we think of all these barriers, we may wonder if it is *possible* to communicate effectively with others. There are numerous things each of us can do to ensure healthy communication. Let us take a look at some of them.

WHAT ARE SOME RESPONSES TO FACILITATE CONSTRUCTIVE COMMUNICATION?

One of the most important components of good communication is attentive listening. When we listen carefully we are saying to the speaker, "You are an important person and I care about what you are saying" (Combs et al., 1971).

Listening means more than just being attentive to the words being spoken (Combs et al., 1971: 270). It also means being alert to our friend's, neighbor's, family member's, or service provider's nonverbal communications. This is what some term "listening with the third ear" (Combs et al., 1971) and it helps us understand the true meaning of what the person is trying to tell us.

When we respond to our family member, friend, or neighbor with warmth, understanding, empathy, support and acceptance, he or she may share in greater depth and with a higher level of trust (Johnson, 1972: 86; Greenberg et al., 1976; Herr and Weakland, 1979; Eriksen, 1979). These responses convey that we will accept the speaker no matter what he or she has done or feels, that we are attempting to understand by trying to put ourselves in his or her shoes, and we will attempt to offer support and realistic encouragement to the person communicating with us. These responses are needed by persons especially in times of crisis, conflict, or indecision (Eriksen, 1979).

Describing one's feelings to others can be a positive form of communication. This may begin a conversation that can improve a relationship with another person as well as help a person to become more aware of what he or she actually feels (Johnson, 1972). When talking about your feelings, you may find it more helpful to describe them than to express them through value judgments. For example, it will be more helpful to say, "I feel frustrated because Dad wouldn't talk about the issues I felt were important" than to say, "Talking with Dad this morning was a complete waste of time for me."

In the role as a listener, it is helpful to reflect the feelings you think you have heard the other person share. This is difficult to do because not only do you need to listen to the content of the words, but you need to go beyond the words to try to determine the feelings being expressed (Greenberg et al., 1976). The way in which the speaker says something is very important in understanding his or her feelings. Here again, nonverbal cues are important in tuning in to the feelings being expressed. Here is an example of reflecting the speaker's feelings (Greenberg et al., 1976: 51):

> Older Person: "I don't know why my daughter didn't come to visit me today; she promised she would."
>
> Listener: "You're *upset* that your daughter didn't come to visit today."

If you have a difficult time identifying the speaker's feelings, it might be helpful to follow your instincts or to try your best guess (Greenberg et al., 1976). Or it may help first to try to put yourself in the other person's position and then to try to determine how you would feel. When reflecting another person's feelings, it is important to respond in a tentative manner, as if you do not really know what feeling he or she is trying to express. You are trying to understand his or her situation, so you need to obtain his or her response as to whether you are really understanding. You may wish to begin your statements with "It seems to me that you are . . ." or "It sounds like you are . . ." (Greenberg et al., 1976).

Although reflecting others' feelings can further communication, it can also become artificial and unnatural. There is no right or wrong way to do it. *It will be most useful for you to find a style compatible with your natural communication patterns, keeping in mind your goal to develop a deeper understanding of what the speaker is attempting to communicate with you.*

Simplicity is another thing to keep in mind as you work toward clear and constructive communication. The simpler the material is, the easier it will be comprehended (Combs et al., 1971). Obviously, this is a relative matter; what is simple for one person may not be for another. As you communicate with another person, it is important to keep in mind his or her life experiences and educational background.

We all select what we perceive. It is impossible to absorb everything that is communicated to us (Combs et al., 1971). Therefore, we take in the information we want and need to absorb. It is not enough that the information seems important to the person who is talking, but the person who is listening must also have a need for or interest in it (Combs et al., 1971). If you want to communicate information to someone, you may first want to think through how or if it is relevant to his or her current interests or problems. For example, you would not want to give instructions to your mother about her new medication and expect her to follow them on her own when you are aware she is consumed with grief for a friend who died yesterday. She likely would not absorb the information.

Sometimes you may make the judgment that the older family member is not ready to deal with certain pieces of information. You decide to withhold the information. Although you are well-meaning and do not want to "hurt" your relative, your action may be more harmful to the person by depriving him or her of the opportunity to make a decision on his or her own behalf (Combs et al., 1971). This may also cheat the older family member of his or her independence. *It is important to relay all appropriate information in an understanding way to your older family member.* This may be difficult at times and take a great deal of time and patience (Combs et al., 1971).

Appropriate responses to conflict can also promote good communication. No relationship will be without periods of conflict (Johnson, 1972). The way in which conflict is handled is very important in building and maintaining relationships (Johnson, 1972). If you are in conflict, you may need to express anger and other emotions in order to clear the air. As you express these emotions, it is helpful to express them with personal statements using "I," "me," or "my." Try not to make accusations and judgments about or commands to the other person(s) involved. Your willingness to communicate these emotions openly and positively shows the importance of the relationship to you. The outcome of working out conflict positively may range from completely alleviating the conflict, to you and the other person(s) "agreeing to disagree." Once you "agree to disagree," you may be able to turn your attention to something else (Herr and Weakland, 1979).

CONCLUSION

In this chapter we have discussed barriers that may keep us from having positive communication experiences as well as responses to facilitate positive experiences. In the next chapter we will cover factors to consider as a caregiver communicates with older people, communication within a family context, and specific communication experiences a caregiver may be involved in as he or she fulfills the responsibilities of a caregiver. These include communicating through the life review process, communicating with a stroke victim and with persons diagnosed with a dementing illness, and communicating with service providers.

SUGGESTIONS FOR PRACTICE

1. Present a community education program on communication. Discuss the differences between verbal and nonverbal communication. Emphasize how to use verbal and nonverbal communication in providing care for a dependent older person.

2. Develop a workshop on communication for family caregivers. Invite caregivers and other service providers who work with dependent older persons. Discuss the barriers that inhibit good communication as well as ways to overcome these barriers.

3. Develop information materials illustrating good communication. Distribute these materials in hospitals, doctors' offices, senior centers, and other public places where family caregivers might see them.

4. Write an article for a local newspaper on communication with a dependent older person. Give ways to enhance the communication process. In

some communities, a "Tips for Caregivers" column could become a regular part of the newspaper.

RESOURCE LIST

To obtain additional information about communication you may want to explore the following resources.

Books

Egan, G. (1976). *Interpersonal living.* Monterey, CA: Brooks/Cole.

Galvin, K. M., & Brommel, B. J. (1982). *Family communication: Cohesion and change.* Glenview, IL: Scott, Foresman.

Greenberg, L., Fatula, B., Hameister, D. R., & Hickey, T. (1976). *Communication skills for the gerontological practitioner.* University Park: Pennsylvania State University.

Kumin, L. (1978). *Aphasia.* Lincoln, NB: Cliff Notes.

Millar, D. P., & Millar, F. E. (1976). *Messages and myths.* Washington, NY: Alfred.

Oyer, H. J., & Oyer, E. J. (1976). *Aging and communication.* Baltimore: University Park Press.

Scoresby, A. L. (1977). *The marriage dialogue.* Reading, MA: Addison-Wesley.

Tamir, L. M. (1979). *Communication and the aging process.* New York: Pergamon.

Chapter 6

POTENTIAL COMMUNICATION EXPERIENCES FOR THE CAREGIVER

Key Questions

1. What are some factors to consider when communicating with older persons?
2. What is involved in communication experiences within a family context?
3. How may life review provide a positive communication experience for an older family member and his or her caregiver?
4. What should a caregiver do as he or she communicates with a stroke victim?
5. How can a caregiver communicate with someone who has been diagnosed with a dementing illness?
6. How may reality orientation techniques assist with communication?
7. What are some things caregivers should know as they communicate with service providers?

In this chapter we will continue our discussion of communication. In Chapter 5 we looked at general communication skills. We will focus on specific communication experiences. These include factors to consider when communicating with older people, communication within a family context, life review with older family members, communicating with a stroke victim, communicating with persons diagnosed with a dementing illness, and communicating with service providers.

WHAT ARE SOME FACTORS TO CONSIDER IN COMMUNICATING WITH OLDER PEOPLE?

In Chapter 5 we discussed that communication is important for everyone. It may become even more important for older persons as they experience a loss of roles and significant relationships (Oyer and Oyer, 1976: 1). It is crucial that opportunities for communication be available to them in order to promote their feelings of self-worth. The *amount* of interaction an older person will have may vary according to his or her physical and emotional health. Some older family members will not be able physically or emotionally to communicate with others for long periods. However, *it is very important for other people to spend meaningful time with them so they know they are important persons.*

There are a number of factors to keep in mind when communicating with older people.

Life Experiences

An older family member has accumulated many life experiences that make him or her a unique person (Tamir, 1979). He or she may be interested in communicating about some things because of those experiences and disinterested in other things. His or her life experiences will also shape the manner in which he or she communicates with other people.

Sensory Changes

Sensory changes may accompany the normal aging process. These changes can affect the way in which an older person perceives and adapts to his or her environment. These changes can obstruct successful communication (Tamir, 1979). For example, if an older family member has a profound hearing loss, the caregiver will need to communicate much differently with him or her than if the older person hears well (see Table 6.1). When relating to someone with sensory changes it is important to compensate for the loss(es).

Health-Related Factors

Other health-related factors could affect communication with older adults. An older family member may become fatigued easily. As a result, a caregiver may have mistakenly evaluated him or her as behaving passively or disinterested when in fact he or she was just responding more slowly (Tamir, 1979). A caregiver needs to be sensitive to times when communication becomes too demanding for an older relative. You may need to postpone talking with him or her so he or she can rest.

TABLE 6.1
Hearing Changes and Interventions

Hearing losses are more common than visual impairments. Older persons with impaired hearing show lower ability to communicate and to adapt to their environment (Oyer and Oyer, 1976: 8). Hearing loss tends to increase the social isolation of older persons (Oyer and Oyer, 1976: 8). They may be considered by others to be inattentive or "senile" because they answered questions inappropriately, when in fact they couldn't hear what was being said. An older person's hearing should be tested by a professional if any of the following behaviors is observed:

A. Recognizing Hearing Changes*

    1. *Increased volume of speaking:* persons whose speaking voice increases in volume may be suffering from increasing amounts of hearing loss. This is particularly true if there is no apparent reason for speaking more loudly.

    2. *Positioning of head:* If there is hearing loss in one ear, a person may tip his or her head in that direction to compensate.

    3. *Asking for things to be repeated:* apparent confusion over tasks to be accomplished or constant blaming of other persons for not making directions clear

    4. *Blank looks and disorientation:* inappropriate answers

    5. *Isolation:* A common symptom of hearing loss is withdrawal from social participation. A person may refuse to engage in conversation with other people because he or she doesn't want a hearing loss to be recognized.

    6. *Shorter attention span than usual:* may seem to drift off in space or begin to do something else when a person is talking.

    7. *No response to a verbal message or sudden noise.*

    8. *An emotional upset:* a change in the emotional status of the person (e.g., hyperactivity, frustration, anger)

B. Interventions*

    1. Hearing aid (not a "cure-all")

    2. When speaking to someone, gain their attention first. Stand in front of him or her so he or she can see you and/or read lips. You may need to touch the person in order to gain his or her attention.

    3. Use gestures and/or objects that illustrate verbal messages (e.g., if going to another room, point to the room; or if talking about an object, show it to the person)

    4. Use short sentences. The longer the sentence and the more detailed the message, the greater the difficulty in accurately understanding what is being said.

    5. Attempt to speak in the ear that retains the best hearing.

    6. Carry a paper and pencil with you to write messages.

---

*Reprinted with permission from M. Ernst and H. Shore, *Sensitizing People to the Processes of Aging: The In-Service Educator's Guide.* Denton, TX: Center for Studies in Aging, 1975.

Difficulty with mobility will affect the kind and amount of communication an older person can have. If an older relative is confined to bed or to one room, he or she can easily be cut off from the mainstream of activity (Oyer and Oyer, 1976) and the normal flow of a family conversation (Oyer, 1976). Perhaps he or she cannot come to the table to eat and therefore misses a special family sharing time. In these situations it is important to make special and appropriate efforts to take the communication to an older relative rather than expect him or her to come to you. Attention to nonverbal communication presented by an older relative may be especially important here (Greenberg et al., 1976). It may be that he or she is too ill to communicate verbally but gives cues and signals that communicate a variety of things.

Perhaps the most important element in communication with an older person is to find the level where communication can take place and begin there (Hausman, 1979). For example, it will only frustrate you and your older family member if you try to reason with him or her when he or she has lost the ability to reason. This may mean giving up some hopes, but it may also mean giving the kind of affectional support most needed by the older person (Hausman, 1979).

"Dependency"

Decreasing power is a major difficulty for some older adults (Tamir, 1979). The tendency is for the more dominant person to take over the communication role. A daughter may tell the physician what is wrong with her father rather than let her father explain (Bettinghaus and Bettinghaus, 1976). The younger person may control the initiation and amount of interaction with the older adult (Tamir, 1979). Even though he or she may feel angry about being placed in a subordinate position, the older person may not fight it for fear that the other person(s) will end their relationship (Tamir, 1979).

To avoid this situation, *the older person needs to be recognized as a competent participant who makes a useful contribution* (Tamir, 1979). It is important for him or her to remain in control of his or her life as much as is physically and emotionally possible. He or she should be provided with all the information needed to make decisions successfully about his or her life.

A caregiver may want to evaluate any decisions that have been made about an older family member to determine whether they were made for his or her benefit. Be careful in making this evaluation, however. Do not berate yourself if you find you stepped in when your family member should have made his or her own decision. You likely did the best you could with the information and awareness you had at the time. Perhaps you can "retrack" and make changes. Perhaps you cannot make changes at this point. However, this new awareness can determine your future involvement with your older family member as new decisions need to be made.

On the other side of the issue, older persons are sometimes unable to ask for the assistance they need for fear of losing their independence. It may be necessary for a caregiver to encourage a relative to express his or her needs as well as his or her fears about what those needs mean to him or her. *As you communicate your desire and commitment to promote whatever amount of independence is reasonable for him or her, your older family member may feel more free to communicate with you.*

WHAT IS INVOLVED IN COMMUNICATION EXPERIENCES WITHIN A FAMILY CONTEXT?

As a family caregiver, you find yourself communicating with other family members as well as your older dependent family member. Issues regarding the care of an older relative have the potential to affect all family members in one way or another. The way in which a family communicates these issues can make a great deal of difference in the emotional cost to all involved (Oyer and Oyer, 1976).

Each family has its own language—that is, the way in which a family sees and understands things, describes them, and, in general, relates to the world (Herr and Weakland, 1979). Your nuclear family language (including the communication patterns of you, your husband, and children) may differ from the language of your family of orientation (including parents, brothers and sisters). Because the caregiving role often requires communication between members of both groups, this difference may call for special efforts to ensure effective communication.

If you are experiencing difficulties, *it may be that your family has had a long-standing history of communication problems.* Perhaps you and your parent have never gotten along. Or the communication difficulties may just have arisen in this time of crisis (Silverstone and Hyman, 1982). Perhaps you and your husband had a pleasant relationship until your father suffered his stroke.

Families are sometimes unaware of their inability to communicate effectively with each other (Silverstone and Hyman, 1982). They may think their complaining, arguing, and fighting is the best they can do. And perhaps it is the best they can do considering the stress they are under and the communication patterns they are currently using. It is likely that with help in learning more effective means of communicating, the arguing and fighting can diminish and more positive forms of communication will result. At times, professionals (including social workers, family therapists, and pastors) are needed to help a family learn more positive communication skills.

The process of sharing your own thoughts and feelings and inviting other family members involved in the conflict to do the same may be useful. The following examples show how one family member invites another family member to join him or her in attempting to resolve a conflict through open communication:

> *A wife may say to her husband:* "It seems as though I've been spending all of my free time at Mom and Dad's house. I feel really frustrated. . . . I want to help them out, yet I want to spend more time with you too. I've felt that you have been angry with me for being gone so much. How can we manage better?" [adapted from Silverstone and Hyman, 1982: 61].

> *A daughter may say to her mother:* "I know you feel more comfortable if I help you bathe and get ready for bed. And I want to help you with that whenever I can, but I also want to go to Jodi's concert this Friday evening. What changes could we make for this evening?"

Family conferences have also been found to be helpful at times (Silverstone and Hyman, 1982). This serves as an alternative to having only one or two persons making all the decisions. It also provides an opportunity for all family members—including the older person—to communicate their thoughts, feelings, and preferences. The family conference may elicit new insights and new approaches to respond to the situation. The new approaches may not work for some time. It may call for a trial-and-error approach. Relationships, which may change, may feel unnatural for awhile. And family members may slip back into old behavioral patterns. However, in time this approach may help to lessen family strains and may uncover solutions that never occurred to any one person when they were struggling alone (Silverstone and Hyman, 1982).

WHAT ARE SOME UNIQUE COMMUNICATION EXPERIENCES IN THE CAREGIVING SITUATION?

A caregiving situation may include some unique communication experiences. Let us briefly review some of these possible experiences.

Life Review

In Chapter 2 on the overview of the aging process, the life review process was discussed briefly. Now we want to add additional information about life review as an opportunity for communication with older persons. Robert Butler, a geriatric physician, found a life review process to take place almost universally among older adults (Butler, 1968). He believes that through life review, older persons attempt to evaluate their past, decide what they will do with any time left to them, and evaluate whatever emotional and material gifts they may have to give others (Butler, 1975). This may explain why many older persons talk about their past. People who do not understand why this happens sometimes become impatient with older people who seem constantly to be living in the past and they view life review as a negative experience.

For a small number of older persons, especially those who feel sad about the course their life has taken, life review is very painful and difficult. They may respond to this sadness in a depressed manner. In these situations, it may be necessary to contact a professional person (mental health worker, social worker, minister) to help the person bring some resolution to his or her past experiences. Remember, these persons are few in number.

Most persons experiencing life review are also dealing with the present and future and use this as a positive experience (Tamir, 1979). Even for these persons, it is not unusual to feel some grief when reliving the death of loved ones or thinking about their own death. However, these feelings are natural. If an older family member is experiencing these feelings, a caregiver should not be alarmed by them. You can be helpful to an older family member by acknowledging and showing understanding and concern for his or her feelings.

For the majority of older persons who experience life review as a healthy and necessary process, an effective listener does not need extensive training. The person(s) who can be the most helpful express genuine interest and are able to listen empathetically. Family members and friends of the older person can be very helpful as they add their own memories and add insights and support (Lewis and Butler, 1977). A number of methods have been used to facilitate life review with older persons. Table 6.2 presents techniques to encourage life review.

Communicating with a Stroke Victim

Some caregivers may be caring for a stroke victim. His or her stroke may have caused a language impairment called aphasia. Each stroke victim's impairment is different. An older family member's impairments can range

TABLE 6.2
Techniques to Encourage Life Review

1. Oral Histories

Using a set of questions that focus on a specific topic to encourage an older person to "tell the way they remember it" can be helpful.

For example, older persons can be asked to discuss the development of business or transportation in the home town of the older person.

2. Family Trees or Genealogies

Many older persons are interested in their family trees. Sometimes they want to know about their parents and grandparents. One of the ways the old resolve fears of death is to gain a sense of family members who preceded them in death. Visits to genealogy libraries or family cemeteries may be beneficial.

3. Attending Family and/or School Reunions

This allows an older person to see himself or herself in the context of other meaningful people and evaluate where he or she fits into the past.

4. Pilgrimages

Persons have been encouraged to make trips to the location of their births or places of significance to them. Some may "journey" to these significant places through correspondence with friends or conversation with others who have recently visited the significant locations.

5. Discussion of Career or Life's Work

This is especially helpful for persons whose work has been important to them. For some persons without family, this experience may meet the need to feel that their lives are meaningful.

6. Family Pictures, Correspondence, and Other Memorabilia

Careful review of family scrapbooks, picture albums, old letters, and other memorabilia establishes positive rapport and facilitates a pleasant form of interviewing older persons. Also, persons with moderate brain damage can remember details through pictures and other memorabilia.

7. Autobiographies

This is an unthreatening way to open communication with older people.

The older person can write or tape an autobiography

8. Story-Telling about Past

Many older people like to tell stories about the past, and they can be encouraged to describe many things they experience. This may be particularly interesting to grandchildren and other younger people.

9. Interviews for Student Assignments or Scientific Research

In some cases, interviews conducted by students or scientific researchers are helpful in remembering the past. Older persons have a large storehouse of experiences they can share.

NOTE: Some of the above are adopted from Lewis and Butler (1974).

from those so mild that few people detect them to so severe that it is impossible to communicate with him or her either orally or through written language (Kumin, 1978). The way in which a caregiver assists a family member with communication depends on his or her specific difficulty (Mace and Rabins, 1981). A caregiver may find it helpful to contact a stroke rehabilitation team to work with the older family member and to learn how to assist in communicating with him or her. Much has been done to rehabilitate stroke victims (Mace and Rabins, 1981: 30).

Sometimes people relate to a stroke victims as though he or she cannot understand what is being said. They assume that because he or she cannot speak, neither can he or she understand. This frequently is not the case. If this is your experience with an older family member, he or she will likely be very frustrated. You may need to help other people know that your family member *can* understand what they are saying.

Communicating with a Person Diagnosed as Having a Dementing Illness

Some may be caring for a person who has been diagnosed as suffering from a dementing illness. The brain damage brought about by the dementia usually comes gradually and varies from person to person, so that each person's abilities also vary. In fact, an older family member's abilities may fluctuate from day to day or even hour to hour (Mace and Rabins, 1981). This fluctuation makes it difficult to know what to expect and to determine the most helpful ways to respond to a relative.

Several communication problems have been associated with persons suffering from a dementing illness (see Table 6.3). Generally, these include problems the person has in expressing himself or herself to others and problems in understanding what others say to him or her (Mace and Rabins, 1981). A common fear may be that a family member's problems will become worse as time passes. It is not true that all persons become worse; this depends on the specific disease (Mace and Rabins, 1981). For this reason, those relating to a person suffering from a dementing illness will find it helpful to make contact with physicians who are knowledgeable about dementing illnesses in order to learn as much as possible about the family member's illness. Talk with other persons experiencing similar situations and develop a support group to learn how to communicate best with the impaired family member. A volunteer organization named the Alzheimer's Disease and Related Disorders Association (ADRDA) was developed to provide support and information to families of persons suffering from all dementing illnesses, including Alzheimer's disease (Mace and Rabins, 1981). *The 36-Hour Day,* a book by Nancy L. Mace and Peter V. Rabins, provides invaluable information for family caregivers of persons suffering dementing illnesses.

TABLE 6.3
Speech and Communication Problems with
Persons Suffering from Dementing Illness

There are two general types of communication problems for persons suffering from dementing illnesses: (1) problems he or she has in expressing himself or herself to others and (2) problems he or she has in understanding others.

Possible Communication Problems in Expressing Self to Others	*Ways to Help Impaired Person Communicate*
1. Occasional difficulty finding words	
Trouble remembering names of familiar objects or people	Usually less frustrating for him or her to have you supply the word than to let him or her search and struggle
Substitution of words that sound similar ("bat" for "bag")	If you know the word he or she means, it may be helpful to supply correct word. If doing so upsets him or her, best to ignore it. When you don't know the word, ask him or her to describe or point it out
Substitution of words with similar meanings ("picture box" for "TV")	
May describe the object for which he or she has forgotten the name ("thing you put food in" for "refrigerator")	
2. Difficulty communicating thoughts	
Can't communicate whole thought but only a few words	May be able to guess what he or she wants to say. *Ask* if you are guessing correctly. If you guess wrong, you will confuse the person even more
Rambling—will string together commonly used phrases. May seem to make sense but actually does not	Even if person can't communicate verbally, his or her feelings are usually accurate. Respond to feelings (need to be alert to nonverbal cues)

(continued)

TABLE 6.3 Continued

3. In severe cases the person may

remember only a few key words eventually be unable to speak repeat phrases over and over cry out intermittently mumble unintelligible phrases	If person can still shake head, ask simplified questions about his or her needs Establish regular routine of checking his or her comfort. Make sure clothing is comfortable, room is warm, no rashes or sores on skin, taken to toilet on regular schedule, not hungry or sleepy

Family members often grieve when they can no longer verbally communicate with a loved one because of lost companionship

Adopted from Mace and Rabins (1981).

Reality Orientation

Some caregivers may be familiar with the term "reality orientation." This is a rehabilitative technique used with persons experiencing a moderate to severe degree of memory loss and confusion about the time and date of day, where they are, who they are, or who is talking to them (Brody, 1977). Reality orientation involves continually informing the person of such things as

—his or her name
—his or her location
—the time, day, and date
—daily events that occur, such as which meal is being served and the names of the food served
—where he or she is going (to the doctor, to the bathroom, etc.); when he or she is going/how long he or she may be gone; what will happen; and what is expected of him or her [Brody, 1977: 282-283]

Environmental aids are often used to reinforce reality orientation. These include

—a reality orientation board (used to spell out a variety of things including address, date, weather, names of family members, and things that will occur during the day)
—large calendars
—large clocks [Brody, 1977: 283]

If you decide to use reality orientation you will find it to be most effective when all persons relating to an older relative use it (Brody, 1977). When using reality orientation you need to be patient, repeat directions frequently, and confirm that your family member has given correct responses. A goal of reality orientation is to help the family member gain some orientation and to become more self-directing. This may or may not happen, depending on the severity of his or her disorientation. To become impatient with a relative if he or she does not seem to be making progress or to give up too quickly provides no help.

Caution needs to be practiced in diagnosing a need for reality orientation. It cannot be automatically assumed that a person will benefit from reality orientation. A thorough diagnosis is needed to determine whether there are reversible causes for your older relative's confused or disoriented behavior (e.g., over- or undermedication, poor nutrition, or depression). Also, do not treat a relative as a child (Brody, 1977). In addition to being disrespectful, treating a relative like an infant is harmful. A professional skilled in working with disoriented persons can assist in using reality orientation with your family member.

Communicating with Service Providers

As an older family member becomes less able to do things for himself or herself, a caregiver may find it necessary to be in contact with numerous service providers to obtain information and resources. The effectiveness of communication among these service providers, an older family member, and a caregiver may determine the kinds and quality of services received (Oyer and Oyer, 1976).

It is sometimes difficult to communicate with agency personnel. Frequently older persons need the services of more than one agency. Each agency tends to develop its own language and communication systems (Oyer and Oyer, 1976). It often takes time to understand the agencies with which you are working. Do not hesitate to ask questions about things you do not understand. As a consumer of these services, you have a right to information about the agency and how it may affect your life.

There may be times when you feel the agency is not meeting your older family member's specific needs. At times the client's needs may be assessed according to the needs of the agency (Shanas and Sussman, 1977). When this is done, the client's needs may be overlooked. If you feel this is happening, share your thoughts with the agency personnel. You and your older family member have a right to be involved in the decisions that are made about the services given to you.

As you are communicating with agency personnel, also be aware of your right to a range of alternatives. An older family member's needs may not fit neatly into the services that are currently provided. A completely new service or an expanded service may be necessary to meet a family member's unique needs. The agency may not currently be in a position to create new or expanded services. However, it is important for them to be aware of these needs as they plan for future changes.

CONCLUSION

We have covered a great deal of material on communication. The importance of communication has been stressed again and again. Although much of the focus has been on how communication skills can be improved, our hope is that you have also learned how important it is for caregivers to interact with people with whom they can share feelings and receive support. These persons can be family members, friends, neighbors, or service providers. In the next two chapters we will look at how these persons might be supportive. Chapter 7 will focus on informal support systems: family, friends, and neighbors. Chapter 8 will focus on formal support systems—that is community services that may be available to you as a caregiver.

SUGGESTIONS FOR PRACTICE

1. Encourage family caregivers to participate in a life review with the older dependent family members. Develop a pamphlet on how to use life review for positive communication. A workshop on life review may be worthwile.

2. Develop "Tips for Communicating with a Stroke Victim" and publish it in the newspaper. Communicate this information on the radio.

3. Organize a seminar on communicating with service providers. Have professionals from various community agencies outline their services and what one should anticipate if they need the services. Discuss ways to talk with service providers.

COMMUNICATION EXERCISE

Introduction

The material in the last two chapters has focused on communication in the family. Primary attention has been focused on communication between the caregiver and older family member. This exercise includes a number of questions concerning the caregiver's relationship with an older person. The primary objective is to assist the caregiver in closely examining his or her communication patterns with his or her older person. Answer each question as it applies to your specific caregiving situation.

Questions

1. Caregivers communicate both verbally and nonverbally. As a caregiver think of several communication experiences you had today. What did you communicate nonverbally? Was it consistent with the things you expressed verbally? If not, think about what the message was that you really wanted to convey. How might you change your verbal or nonverbal messages to relay that message in a consistent manner?
2. How might you express the following messages nonverbally?
   I really care about you.
   I feel angry with you.
   I'd like for you to feel free to share your feelings with me.
3. If a family member is no longer able to be in the normal flow of conversation within your household, how might you and other family members, friends, and neighbors "take the conversation" to him or her?
4. How have you needed to adjust your communication expectations to meet the needs of your family member as he or she became less able to care for himself or herself? What has helped you change your expectations? How do you feel about these changes?
5. As a caregiver, what compensations have you needed to make as you communicate with an older family member whose senses are not as acute as they were? What have you found to be helpful?
6. In what ways have you encouraged your older family member to remain as independent as possible even though he or she has grown more dependent on you?
7. Do you recognize any barriers to good communication frequently practiced in your family? How might you eliminate these barriers?
8. What responses does your family practice that promote good communication?
9. What frustrations have you had in communicating with your older family member? What have you found to be helpful in working with these frustrations? What frustrations would you like the group to help you with?

Chapter 7

INFORMAL SUPPORT SYSTEMS

Key Questions

1. Why is a support system important?
2. What are the different kinds of support included in support systems?
3. For what reasons do persons not receive support?
4. What is an informal support system?
5. For what reasons should we consider receiving support from informal support systems?
6. How may family members provide support?
7. How may friends provide support?
8. How may neighbors provide support?
9. How may churches provide support?
10. What are the limitations of informal support systems?

When you think of yourself as a caregiver, a question you may ask *often* is this: "What kind of support does my older family member need?" However, you *seldom* ask this question: "What kind of support do *I* need?" The second question is as important as the first and is our focus of discussion in this chapter.

It may be difficult for caregivers to allow themselves to think about what they need from others. It may seem very selfish. If you are feeling this way, our hope is that you will think about the support you need in the caregiver role. In this chapter we will look at informal support systems, including how family, friends, and neighbors can be helpful to the caregiver role. In the next chapter we will consider available formal supports including services offered by public and private agencies.

WHY IS A SUPPORT SYSTEM IMPORTANT?

Support is something all people need regardless of their caregiving activities—it is a basic human need. We all need support. For our purposes we will define support as any physical, emotional, financial, or spiritual elements that help sustain us through the difficult times in our lives. Most people develop a sense of well-being by developing supportive relationships with others (Caplan, 1974). These supportive persons help us respond to the challenges and strains in our lives (Caplan, 1974). Evidence shows that persons who offer support help us keep our emotional and physical health.

Support is especially important when persons are experiencing transitions and stress. At these times support systems that were developed earlier (usually spontaneously) could be inadequate (Waters et al., 1980). A person involved in long-term, stressful situations runs a higher risk of illness unless a planned support system to "fill the gaps" is initiated (Caplan, 1974). With the preceding information, we can see that developing support systems for a caregiver is not selfish but is a way to enable the caregiver to take better care of an older dependent family member. Because a relative's well-being depends on the caregiver's well-being, it is essential to find ways to care for the caregiver (Mace and Rabins, 1981). It has been found that caregivers who receive adequate emotional support and physical help with caregiving tasks feel less burdened than those who receive little or no support (Zarit et al., 1980). It would make sense, then, that caregivers who receive adequate support might be able to keep their older family member at home longer.

WHAT ARE THE DIFFERENT KINDS OF SUPPORT INCLUDED IN SUPPORT SYSTEMS?

There are many different kinds of support a person may need at various times throughout their lives. We may need *ongoing* support from significant persons or groups in order to deal with particular long-term burdens or stresses (Caplan, 1974). At other times we may need *intermittent, short-term* support from others in order to deal with an acute need or crisis (Caplan, 1974).

There will be times when we need *instrumental* support from others. Instrumental supports involve obtaining actual physical assistance with necessary tasks, such as running errands or staying with the older family member so the caregiver can relax. At other times *expressive* support is needed. This is support in which a person gives companionship and caring to another person. Some supports can best be offered by an *informal* system including family, friends, and neighbors. Others can best be given by *formal* supports, including doctors, lawyers, and other social service providers.

WHY DO PERSONS SOMETIMES NOT RECEIVE SUPPORT?

There are several reasons why persons do not receive support. Someone may have decided not to ask for it because he or she would not want to appear weak (Caplan, 1974). However, asking for support actually promotes wellness and builds a person's strengths so that he or she might respond appropriately to his or her environment (Caplan, 1974).

Others feel that persons around them should be aware of their needs and should offer help, that they should not have to ask for it (Waters et al., 1980). Even though we may feel someone very close to us should be aware of the stress we are under or should recognize our need for help, he or she may not be so aware. Or if he or she does know our need for help, he or she may not know how to become involved. Perhaps the person is too frightened to ask how to get involved. Or the person may fear he or she will not be able to give the kind of support needed. In some situations, *a caregiver will need to help others know how they can be helpful.*

Sometimes caregivers ask for help and friends and family do not respond (Mace and Rabins, 1981). If a caregiver does not have understanding friends, if a family is not willing to help, if the person who is being cared for refuses to stay with anyone else, or if a caregiver cannot afford outside help, it may seem impossible to find the support needed (Mace and Rabins, 1981). Finding other means of support may take the effort the caregiver feels he or she does not have. However, the support is so necessary that it *must* be found (Mace and Rabins, 1981). Perhaps a caregiver can piece together a patchwork of supports in order to get all that is needed. For example,

> Mr. Cooke persuaded the day care center to take his wife one day a week by agreeing to teach the staff how to manage her. His son, who lived out of state, agreed to pay for the day care. His neighbor agreed to come over and help get his wife dressed on those mornings [Mace and Rabins, 1981: 175].

Caregivers may also need to accept a plan that is not exactly what they would like (Mace and Rabins, 1981). They may not be totally satisfied with the care others give an older family member on their days off. They may need to make some financial sacrifices. *It is important for a caregiver, if at all possible, to be persistent in searching for help, keeping in mind that he or she may need to make some compromises with the respite plan he or she would most like to have* (Mace and Rabins, 1981). *Most of all, keep in mind that it's OK to ask for support!!*

WHAT IS AN INFORMAL SUPPORT SYSTEM?

As we discuss informal support systems we will be focusing on family members, friends, and/or neighbors who provide emotional and physical support to family caregivers. This assistance allows the caregiver to keep his or her older dependent family member at home longer than would otherwise be the case. The persons providing the assistance may do such things as stay with the dependent family member so the caregiver can get away for relaxation and to run errands, share the caregiver's frustrations and problems, visit with the caregiver and/or older family member, share the caregiving tasks, run errands, provide financial or other material assistance, help with household tasks or minor home repair tasks, or provide skills or guidance in responding to bewildering situations.

WHY SHOULD WE CONSIDER RECEIVING SUPPORT
FROM INFORMAL SUPPORT SYSTEMS?

It is important to help family members, friends, and neighbors know how to be effectively involved with the older dependent family member because most older persons are already tied into this network in some way (Lebowitz, 1978). This is the most natural support to seek because it provides the older person and caregiver with opportunities to continue relating to persons to whom they have related for most of their lives. The emotional attachments of family and friends cannot be easily duplicated by formal service providers (Tobin and Kulys, 1980).

Although family, friends, and neighbors cannot respond to every need of the older family member, they are in many ways the most effective and efficient respondants to the needs of older adults and are often the most welcome helpers (Ward, 1978). Let us look at ways in which they can be helpful.

HOW MAY OTHER FAMILY MEMBERS PROVIDE SUPPORT?

The kind of help a family tends to give their older dependent family member and his or her primary caregiver will vary according to the specific circumstances and previous history of helping each other (Cicirelli, 1981). The family's history of relating to each other will also affect each member's willingness to be involved in the older person's care (Silverstone and Hyman, 1982). For example, if a brother never felt accepted by his father, he may be reluctant to help provide actual physical care for dad now. On the other hand, a sister may want very much to help with father's care to repay the many things she felt he has given her.

As caregivers think about other members of their families who might help care for an older family member, *they need to keep their family history in mind.* Family history cannot be rewritten (Silverstone and Hyman, 1982). Situations may have caused wounds between brother and sister, spouses, parent and children, aunt and nephew, or grandparent and grandchild. Relationships in which there has been a long history of tension cannot easily be turned around. However, attitudes and perspectives can be changed slightly and problems may be approached in ways that make them easier to resolve (Silverstone and Hyman, 1982). It may be that old wounds and misunderstandings will need to be dealt with before some family members will offer to help care for an older family member.

*It is important to keep in mind the older family member's independence as a caregiver helps others get involved with his or her care.*Check with the older family member about another person's involvement. He or she should be involved as much as possible in any decisions made concerning his or her care. When others do become involved, help them to consider an older family member's need for as much independence as possible.

In Chapters 7 and 8 we discuss in a general way how family members, friends, and neighbors may be helpful to caregivers. As a caregiver, you will need to take this information and tailor it to your own situation. If you are an adult child of the older person requiring care, sisters and brothers may be able to give a great deal of help. Often parents prefer that their children rather than other family or friends help with their care (Cantor, 1979). Studies of different groups of adult child caregivers have shown that they were better able to cope when their brothers and sisters were also actively involved in the parent's care (Brandwein and Postoff, 1980). When there were no siblings or the siblings did not help in the parent's care, the adult child who served as the primary caregiver suffered the most.

Brothers and sisters may be helpful with both emergency assistance and in long-range commitments (Cantor, 1979). A caregiver may make arrangements to call them on short notice for any emergency situations, such as having one of them stay with a parent while the caregiver picks up a sick child from school. Or someone may develop an ongoing schedule with one or several siblings to share with bathing and transporting a parent to the doctor or day care center. One sibling may stay with a parent one or two days each week so the caregiver can spend time with friends or run errands. Sibling(s) may also visit regularly with a parent, or may make a financial commitment to the care of an older parent so all of the parent's bills do not fall on the caregiver. They may be helpful in contacting social service agencies about services an older family member wishes to utilize (Shanas and Sussman, 1977). In addition, a caregiver may find sibling(s) helpful in sharing the frustrations and joys experienced as he or she cares for a parent. He or she may give some helpful insights as to reasons a parent may be responding in a certain way or how to respond better to some of the parent's behavior.

Other family members who may be helpful are the older family member's siblings. A caregiver may not think of these relatives as being helpful because they too may be old or disabled. Indeed, any physical disabilities they experience may limit the kinds of instrumental support they can give. However, they can provide great emotional support to an older family member and caregiver.

About 80% of all older people have living brothers and sisters. It appears that as persons get older they tend to revive relationships developed earlier with their siblings (Ragan, 1979). Additionally, the more narrow an older person's social world becomes, the more likely he or she is to seek the support of siblings. An older family member may want to see his or her brothers and sisters. The caregiver could arrange for them to come for regular visits. The time they visit together may give the caregiver additional time to himself or herself.

Depending on their own physical well-being, an older family member's siblings may wish to be involved more extensively with his or her care. Perhaps they have wanted to be involved but did not want to interfere and so have not asked to be more involved. They may be limited because of lack of transportation. A caregiver may want to ask an older family member's siblings if and how they would like to help in his or her care. The caregiver, siblings, and older family member can try to find mutually satisfying ways for their involvement.

Other kin, including an older family member's grandchildren, cousins, nieces and nephews, may also offer support (Troll et al., 1979). Their involvement may be based more on their individual characteristics than on the closeness of kinship (Troll et al., 1979). For example, they may want to help not because they feel close kinship ties to an older family member but because they enjoy relating to older people and would enjoy getting to know him or her better. Or they may have been interested in doing some volunteer work and would find helping a rewarding experience. Some of these persons may be willing to be involved only in emergency situations; others may be interested in being involved on a long-term basis.

A caregiver's own family members may offer direct support as well by helping with physical tasks, such as cleaning the house, cooking meals, providing transportation, and running errands. They may provide emotional support by listening to caregiving experiences, offering empathy and understanding for the difficult times, offering helpful insights and possible solutions to frustrating situations, and listening and accepting the caregiver as he or she expresses joy or anger, frustration, and sorrow about the caregiving experiences.

In summary, *the enduring quality of family relationships suggest that family members may be able to detect a caregiver's needs as well as the older family member's needs and can respond with individualized care.* It also suggests that family members may be more likely to "hang-in" consistently with the caregiver and older relative through long-term needs for assistance (Back, 1979). Family members can be a major tie to the community for both the older family member and the caregiver (Shanas, 1979a). For this reason, *the need for regular and supportive family visitors to both an older family member and caregiver is important.*

HOW MAY FRIENDS PROVIDE SUPPORT?

A caregiver's friends and friends of your older family member can provide support. In some instances friends may substitute for the unavailability of family members, or they may offer additional support to that given by family members (Troll et al., 1979; Cantor, 1979).

There may be some important socialization and support tasks that only friends can fulfill (Cantor, 1979). Most social life at all ages is with friends (Troll et al., 1979). Given that friendships are developed by mutual consent rather than prescribed, as are family relationships, continued friendships seem to promote higher moral among persons (Ragan, 1979; Tamir, 1979). This is especially important for older persons who are losing some contact with the outside world. Maintaining contact with friends will provide opportunities for an older family member to share with a confidant. He or she will be able to maintain his or her social role of friend during a time of diminishing roles. Friendships also tend to be more of a reciprocal relationship than are kinship relationships. An older family member may feel he or she is giving as much in the relationships with his or her friends as he or she is receiving, whereas with a caregiver, he or she may feel constantly on the receiving end.

The time an older family member can spend with friends will not only provide emotional and perhaps physical support for him or her but will provide indirect emotional support for the caregiver. For example, the caregiver may be able to spend some time by himself or herself while an older family member's friends are visiting. The increased morale an older family member experiences because of involvement with friends will increase the potential for a positive relationship between the caregiver and him or her.

It may take some effort to enable an older family member's friends to visit him or her. Depending on the age of the family member, he or she may have lost a number of friends through death. Others of his or her friends may be disabled in some way and cannot easily come to visit. However, because friendships are so important, it will be well worth the effort to encourage even a few of the older family member's friends visit him or her regularly. It has been found that even one intimate friend seems to serve as a defense against social losses related to age (Ward, 1978). If the older person no longer has old friends around, caregivers may want to find ways to introduce him or her to new friends.

A caregiver needs the support of good friends to help through the rough times (Mace and Rabins, 1981). With increased caregiving responsibilities, a caregiver may find himself or herself more and more isolated from friends. You must find ways to continue to have friends and social contacts. Your friends may be fearful of what is happening to your older family member and hesitate to visit. They may not feel free to drop by unannounced as they used to for fear of interfering with your schedule. You may need to help them understand the situation and help them know how they can be an important part of your life. You may need to make new friends at a time when all your energy is being used for caregiving responsibilities. If you can start by finding one small resource for yourself, this may give enough energy to find others (Mace and Rabins, 1981).

In summary, friends can be helpful in many ways. Among other things, they can handle the unpredictable; provide emotional support; help to increase an older family member's and a caregiver's morale; provide information; relieve some caregiving tasks; help in times of emergency; be involved in social, recreational, or spiritual activities; or help with transportation (Cicirelli, 1981; Lebowitz, 1978).

HOW MAY NEIGHBORS PROVIDE SUPPORT?

Probably the first characteristic we think about when describing neighbors is proximity. Neighbors usually interact directly (Litwak and Szelenyi, 1969). Studies have shown that neighbors are often helpful in emergency situations and in checking with older persons on a regular basis (Ward, 1978). Neighbors have also been found to be helpful in times of illness by stopping in to check on the ill person, running errands, and helping with transportation (Cantor, 1979). They have served as contacts with the outside world. In one study persons stated that their neighbors provided help with protection, homemaking, transportation, psychological support, and social and recreational activities (Cicirelli, 1981).

Obviously, the involvement of neighbors varies. This will depend on how well a caregiver knows his or her neighbors, whether they live in a rural or urban area, how many families are known in the neighborhood, how long others have lived in the neighborhood, and individual characteristics of the caregiver and his or her neighbors. In general, it appears that neighbors' involvement with caregivers is not as extensive as in the involvement of family and friends (Cantor, 1979). However, many neighbors want to be and are involved with helping their older neighbors and family caregivers.

HOW MAY CHURCHES PROVIDE SUPPORT?

One last component of the informal support system is the church. Ideally, churches should be able to respond to caregivers with spiritual, emotional, and physical support. The church is most often seen as a setting where friendships are built (Steinitz, 1981). Some churches effectively respond to short-term crises requiring emergency food, housing, or personal care services. In some instances churches have blended aspects of both formal organizations and informal support systems (Steinitz, 1981). This has resulted in a flexible neighborhood support where most of the services are informally designed by and for the members.

Perhaps a caregiver's church is not currently organized to respond to the needs of a caregiver. However, there may be persons in the congregation who would like to help but who are unaware of the specific needs. They may want a caregiver to share his or her needs with them. Several church members wrote of how their church responded to their needs:

> We have a 101-year old [bedridden] member living with her nephew about five blocks from the church. When her nephew had to be suddenly hospitalized for his heart condition last Christmas, we organized a 24-hour watch over Mrs. F, caring for all her needs. This lasted four days and four nights. . . . and meant that she didn't have to be institutionalized during that period.

> For transportation I always call the church. I didn't want to at first, because I thought it would be too much trouble. But my friends convinced me. "What is a church for," they said, "if you can't call when you need help?" [Steinitz, 1981: 47].

SUMMARY OF THE IMPORTANCE OF INFORMAL SUPPORT SYSTEMS

A caregiver may feel uncomfortable with our discussion about what family, friends, neighbors, and churches can do as he or she provides care for an older family member. However, studies have shown that primary caregivers feel less burden and more often view their situation as manageable when other members of the dependent older person's informal support system are also involved in care (Zarit et al., 1980). Enhancing a caregiver's informal support system also means enhancing an older family member's informal support system—that is a plus for him or her as well.

Although we have been talking about what others can *do* for a caregiver, we want to acknowledge that caregivers are also *giving* to those in a support system. You are offering much through your relationship with them. You are giving them opportunities to be needed—we all need that. It is important to remember that it is OK to ask for and need support!

WHAT ARE THE LIMITATIONS OF
INFORMAL SUPPORT SYSTEMS?

Although informal support systems are mandatory in enabling a caregiving situation, *the informal supports cannot do it all.* Sometimes formal supports are more suitable (Schmidt, 1981). Relatives and friends may find it more and more difficult to provide certain kinds of care (Schmidt, 1981). *It is erroneous to assume that the best solution for the care of all dependent elderly.is home care* (Fengler and Goodrich, 1979) *or to assume that no social service agencies should ever be involved in an older family member's care.* In the next chapter we will focus on the social services that are available to caregivers. We will learn what services they have to offer and look at how those services may further relieve the burdens of a caregiver.

SUGGESTIONS FOR PRACTICE

1. Form a group of caregivers and discuss various individuals they have helping them provide assistance. Then explore other persons who might be able to help them. Discuss the differences between the informal and formal support systems and ways to encourage people in the informal system to provide assistance.

2. Encourage caregivers to hold family conferences on a periodic but regular basis. The caregivers should invite all members of their informal support system to the conference. Topics discussed by the participants can include needs of dependent older persons, needs of primary caregivers, schedules of participants, and ways some of the participants might help the caregiver. The meeting could be similar to a quarterly report on the progress and problems of the caregiving relationship.

3. Urge the caregivers to consider the advantages and disadvantages of having others help them. Similar to any human relationship, there are rewards and costs involved in receiving assistance. Caregivers may want to weigh the rewards and costs to help decide who they want to ask to help them.

4. Give caregivers the Informal Support System and Kinds of Needs Exercise. Discuss the needs they have and ways to match these needs with persons in the informal support system.

EXERCISE:
INFORMAL SUPPORT SYSTEM
AND KINDS OF NEEDS EXERCISE

Caregivers have a number of people who are a part of an informal support system. The persons can provide assistance in meeting needs of a caregiver and/or older family member. The primary objectives of this exercise are *to identify members of your informal support system and match these persons with your needs in caregiving.*

There are three parts to this exercise. Part 1 focuses on identification of persons in your informal support network. Part 2 asks you to identify the kind of assistance you need in the caregiving role. Part 3 encourages you to match these needs with the persons identified as members of your informal support system.

Identification of Informal Support Systems Exercise

We have talked at length about the importance of receiving support from other family members, friends, and neighbors. Perhaps there are persons you have not thought of who would like to help you with some caregiving tasks. This exercise is designed to provide an opportunity to begin thinking of those persons.

Instructions:

1. On the first worksheet—(7-1) PERSONS WHO MIGHT GIVE YOU SUPPORT/ASSIST-ANCE—list the names of persons in each category who are already supporting you or who you think may want to support you. There is one worksheet for your relatives, friends, and neighbors and one for you to list your older family member's relatives, friends, and neighbors. If these are the same for both of you, complete only one worksheet.
2. On the second worksheet—(7-2) KINDS OF ASSISTANCE NEEDED/DESIRED—list the actual help you would like. Be as specific as you can. Examples are given.
3. On the third worksheet—(7-3) INFORMAL SUPPORT SHEET—combine the information from the first two worksheets. First, list a person's name and then list the kind of support you are already receiving from him or her or think he or she would be willing to provide for you. You will notice there

is also a column for you to list needs or support you think cannot be met by informal supports. We will use that list again during the next session as we discuss formal supports that might help you meet those needs.

4. Please bring these worksheets back next session. After our discussion on formal supports, each of you will be asked to develop an Action Plan to respond to your own situation.

Notes to Leader:

1. As members are filling out worksheets, encourage them to recall and discuss how they developed supports in the past. Once these past "accessing skills" are identified, it may be easier to plan a strategy for building up current supports (Waters et al., 1980).

2. Encourage people to think about how they ask for support and also to think about telling the identified others that they are considered a source of support. Discuss. (Waters et al., 1980).

Part 1   WORKSHEET 7-1

Who are the members of your informal support system? Name the people who might provide you with assistance in caregiving?

1. *Family*
(A) *Children*   (D) *Brothers*   (G) *Nieces*

_____   _____   _____

_____   _____   _____

_____   _____   _____

(B) *Grandchildren*   (E) *Aunts*   (H) *Nephews*

_____   _____   _____

_____   _____   _____

_____   _____   _____

(C) *Sisters*   (F) *Uncles*   (I) *Other Relatives*

_____   _____   _____

_____   _____   _____

_____   _____   _____

_____   _____   _____

2. Nonfamily
(A) *Friends*   (C) *People at Church or Civic Group*

_____   _____
_____   _____
_____   _____

(B) *Neighbors*   (D) *Other*

_____   _____
_____   _____
_____   _____

Part 2   WORKSHEET 7-2

*What are the kinds of assistance you need to fulfill your role as caregiver?
List the specific tasks you think need assistance.*

(A) Physical care of relative   (C) Transportation
    (bathing, lifting, etc.)   _____
    _____   _____
    _____   _____
    _____   _____
    _____   _____
    _____   _____
    _____   _____
    _____   _____

(B) Minor household tasks
    (cooking/cleaning)   (D) To help emotional well-being
    _____   of older family member
    _____   (visiting, asking for advice
    _____   or help)
    _____
    _____   _____
    _____   _____
    _____   _____
    _____   _____
    _____   _____

(E) Minor home repair or
maintenance (painting, fix
storm door, remove
storm windows)

_____

_____

_____

_____

_____

_____

_____

_____

_____

(F) To help emotional well-being
of caregiver (visiting, respite)

_____

_____

_____

_____

_____

_____

(G) Other

_____

_____

_____

_____

Part 3   WORKSHEET 7-3

Who in your support system can help you meet your caregiving needs? Match the names in Part 1 with the needs in Part 2.

(A) Persons who might give you
support/assistance

_____

_____

_____

_____

_____

_____

_____

_____

_____

_____

(B) Kinds of support/assistance

_____

_____

_____

_____

_____

_____

_____

_____

_____

_____

_____

(C) Needs that can't be filled by
      informal supports

_____

_____

_____

_____

_____

_____

_____

_____

RESOURCE LIST

In order to obtain additional information about informal support systems,
you may want to explore the following resources:

Journals

Brubaker, T. H., & Brubaker, E. (1981). Adult child and elderly parent household:
Issues in stress for theory and practice. *Alternative Lifestyles, 4,* 242-256.

Cantor, M. (1979). Neighbors and friends—An overlooked resource in the informal
support system. *Researh on Aging, 1,* 434-463.

The Gerontologist (1983). Symposium: Aging and the family. Informal support systems. *32* (February).

Johnson, C. L., & Catalano, D. J. (1981). Childless elderly and their family supports.
The Gerontologist, 21 (6), 610-618.

Petty, B. J., Moeller, T. P., & Campbell, R. Z. (1976). Support groups for elderly
persons in the community. *The Gerontologist, 15*(6), 522-528.

Schmidt, M. G. (1981). Personal networks: Assessment, care and repair. *Journal of
Gerontological Social Work, 3*(4), 65-70.

Steinitz, D. Y. (1981). The local church as support for the elderly. *Journal of Gerontological Social Work, 4*(2), 43-53.

Wentowski, G. J. (1981). Reciprocity and the coping strategies of older people: Cultural dimensions of network building. *The Gerontologist, 21,* 600-609.

Books

Caplan, G. (1974). *Support systems and community mental health.* New York: Behavioral Publications.

Cicirelli, V. G. (1981). *Helping elderly parents: The role of adult children.* Auburn House.

Chapter 8

FORMAL SUPPORT SYSTEMS

Key Questions

1. What are formal supports?
2. For what reasons should we consider receiving support from formal support systems?
3. What are some limitations of formal supports?
4. What kinds of feelings might you have as you relate to community agencies?
5. What might happen if you can no longer care for your older family member at home?
6. What formal supports may be helpful to you?

In Chapter 7 we discussed the importance of sufficient caregiver support so that some of the burdens of caregiving may be relieved or at least lessened. We focused on how other family, friends, and neighbors (informal supports) might provide support. In this chapter we will look at formal supports that might be helpful. Following our discussion of formal supports, caregivers will have an opportunity to develop an Action Plan they think would offer the best care for them and their older family member. We hope that this exercise and the information in this chapter will alert caregivers to a useful mix of informal and formal supports available to meet their unique caregiving needs. Additional information about this exercise will be given later.

WHAT ARE FORMAL SUPPORTS?

We will be using the term "formal supports" to define community services and agencies designed to assume some of the caregiving tasks for older adults needing them. These services are intended to supplement family care and strengthen the family's ability to respond to the needs of their older family member(s) (Brody, 1979). These formal supports may include medical care, legal services, homemaker services, adult day care centers, nutrition sites, home health services, friendly visitors, telephone reassurance programs, mental health services, transportation services, support groups, and financial assistance programs.

WHY SHOULD WE CONSIDER RECEIVING SUPPORT FROM FORMAL SUPPORT SYSTEMS?

Informal supports are necessary to enable a caregiving situation, but they cannot provide all the support that is needed. At times formal supports are more suitable and/or necessary (Schmidt, 1981). Let us look briefly at some reasons why family caregivers also need formal supports.

Demographics

In recent years family size has decreased. In many cases there are fewer persons within the family unit to provide assistance to the older family member. This suggests a greater burden for those who do serve as caregivers (Munnichs, 1977). In addition to fewer numbers of caregivers, many of the middle-aged women who are also primary caregivers to older adults are now employed outside the home (Brody, 1981). Think of families you know. Are there more women employed outside the home in your generation than there were in your mother's generation? The combined roles of employee and caregiver add stress to the caregiver. One caregiver cannot take care of everything for his or her older family member. If no or few family members, friends, or neighbors are available or willing to help, it is especially important for the caregiver to receive assistance from community services.

Care and Tasks

At times caregiving responsibilities involve specialized skills that family members do not possess (Shanas and Sussman, 1977). For example, unless you are a doctor, you cannot diagnose an illness and prescribe medication. Most people cannot make technical legal decisions without the help of a lawyer. And most cannot practice psychotherapy. Sometimes it is necessary to receive formal support in order to obtain needed expertise and resources.

Service providers may offer this expertise within an objective framework. Sometimes family members are too close to a situation to respond clearly (Mace and Rabins, 1981). Another reason why a caregiver may want to consider using community services is that some are designed to handle the more routine tasks involved in caregiving. Homemaker services is a good example. If someone else is available to assume minor house-cleaning and grocery shopping tasks, a caregiver may have more time and energy to respond to the emotional needs of an older family member.

Independence / Dependence Issues

Sometimes an older family member may feel he or she is losing independence by relying so heavily on other family members (Weihaus, 1979). The older family member may prefer to have some of his or her needs met by formal supports so that he or she still feels somewhat independent of his or her family.

Financial Reasons

Income maintenance programs have enabled families to maintain their elderly relatives in the community as well as lessen their own financial burdens (Moroney, 1976). This has been shown to reduce stress experienced by the family, which, in turn, resulted in more positive relationships among family members (Munnichs, 1977).

WHAT ARE SOME LIMITATIONS
OF FORMAL SUPPORTS?

Formal supports have limitations just as informal supports have limitations. For one thing, formal supports cannot easily respond to the humanistic needs of older people (Atchley, 1983). A service provider will not share your father's, mother's or other relative's family history as you or other family members do. The service provider will not be able to share memories of "the good ole' days" in the neighborhood as a relative's long-time neighbor can. Nor is the service provider likely to drop by frequently for a friendly chat as a close friend might. Although many service providers care a great deal about caregivers and their older family member, because of their professional relationship and responsibilities they often need to maintain some distance.

Another potential limitation of formal support comes from their need to be cost-effective by serving many people. In order to be able to serve many people, a service needs to address generalized rather than individualized needs. A caregiver may request assistance from an agency that appears to serve persons having similar needs but find that because his or her needs are slightly different from those of other clients, the agency cannot be helpful. It may seem that the agency only needs to make a minor adjustment in its services to respond to your needs. However, the agency is unable to make that slight adjustment. You may need to explore several agencies before you find one that responds most satisfactorily to your specific needs.

Once a caregiver becomes involved with an agency, he or she may become discouraged with the seemingly unending bureaucratic "red tape." It may seem that he or she is continually filling out complicated forms or that the rules of the agency are constantly changing.

Another limitation may come with a turnover of personnel in an agency (Moroney, 1976). A caregiver and/or older family member may enjoy relating to a particular service provider. What happens, then, if he or she leaves? The caregiver may have worked with the service provider for a significant length of time and came to know what to expect from him or her, only to have to start at the beginning with a new agency employee. Caregiver and family member may have some fears about whether the new person will be as capable or as nice as the person with whom both had been working. Both may also feel some grief with this loss.

The above limitations may be realities or not, depending on the caregiver's experiences. The limitations have not been discussed to discourage requests for assistance from community services, but rather to highlight the need to develop both informal and formal supports. *One kind of support is not better than another kind. Informal supports can offer some things formal supports cannot. And formal supports can offer some things informal supports cannot.* A caregiver needs a mix of these supports to enhance the caregiving role (Shanas and Sussman, 1977).

WHAT KINDS OF FEELINGS MIGHT A CAREGIVER HAVE AS HE OR SHE RELATES TO COMMUNITY AGENCIES?

It is one thing to involve other family members or friends in personal family affairs, but what about strangers? A caregiver may have mixed feelings, especially in the beginning, about the idea of relating to service providers. On the one hand, the service provider may recognize the caregiver's need for assistance. On the other hand, a caregiver may resist the idea of outsiders becoming aware of any family problems as a result of caregiving responsibilities. The caregiver may resist suggestions these outsiders give. After all, what do they know about what it is *really* like for you and your family? Or you may have fears that these professionals will not really care about your parent or spouse but only relate to him or her so that they can get their paycheck. You may wonder how well trained these outsiders are. Or you may wonder if you can trust them to be in your home with your older family member while you are gone.

It is natural to have mixed feelings about relating to service providers. As a caregiver develops a rapport with the service provider and learns how to work together in a mutually satisfying way, some fears will likely be lessened. On the other hand, if some caregivers cannot work well with the service provider even though he or she has tried to resolve the differences, the caregiver may want to make arrangements for someone else to assume his or her responsibilities.

A caregiver may feel guilty about transferring certain caregiving responsibilities to so-called strangers. These feelings of guilt may surface if an older family member resists the idea of relating to the service provider of a community agency. Some older family members may never understand or accept the need to involve outside agency personnel. If a caregiver struggles with this situation, he or she may need to reconcile this struggle with himself or herself and with the support of other friends, family members, caregivers, or professionals.

WHAT MIGHT HAPPEN IF YOU CAN NO LONGER CARE FOR YOUR OLDER FAMILY MEMBER AT HOME?

Some caregivers come to realize that they are no longer able to care for an older family member at home. This awareness may lead to needing to make one of the most difficult decisions a caregiver will ever have to make: planning a change in the older family member's living arrangements (Goodman, 1980).

In considering relocation of an older family member, a caregiver may experience many different emotions—sadness, fear, uncertainty, frustration, anger, guilt, relief. Experiencing mixed feelings during this process is common

(Goodman, 1980). It may be helpful to share these feelings with others who can offer understanding, acceptance, and helpful insights about the situation. If the caregiver is receiving support from others, he or she can provide more support to the older family member through this traumatic time.

It is likely that a caregiver has a concern that the right decision is made concerning the older family member. An understanding to keep in mind when considering this decision is that *it is very important to be in communication with your older family member about this issue.* After all, this decision has the greatest effect on the older person. Before being told about relocation, it is important for the older person to realize how his or her disabilities are affecting the present living situation. For example, if he or she can see the caregiver's health no longer allows him or her to provide care at home, the older family member may be more willing to look at alternatives (Reuben and Byrnes, 1977).

It is important for the older family member to be as involved as he or she is physically and emotionally able in any decisions that are made concerning him or her (Mace and Rabins, 1981; Yawney and Slover, 1973; Butler and Lewis, 1977; Brody, 1979). Obviously, the amount of involvement an older family member can have in this process will depend on his or her degree of impairment. If a person is too impaired to understand what is happening, it may be better to carry out the plans without involving him or her. Trying to involve an extremely impaired person may cause unnecessary stress (Mace and Rabins, 1981).

The older family member will experience deep emotions through this traumatic time. It is important for him or her to receive emotional support from others. He or she may need to express feelings of fear, anger or frustration, or even relief.

WHAT FORMAL SUPPORTS MAY BE HELPFUL?

The formal supports that will be helpful will depend on the caregiver's informal supports. Each caregiver has his or her own mix of assistance from family friends, neighbors, and community services based on the capacities and needs of the family (Brody, 1979). A caregiver needs to know what community services are available as he or she attempts to respond to an older family member's and his or her own needs. We now explore appropriate services that might be available in your geographic area.

GUIDELINES FOR GATHERING INFORMATION
ABOUT COMMUNITY RESOURCES

It may take a caregiver several weeks or months to gather all the information necessary to know about community resources. It is suggested that caregivers begin planning as soon as they decide to accept the responsibility of caregiving so they will have enough time to gather all relevant information. They may want to collect this material by visiting the agency and meeting with key administrative staff and/or service providers to learn the following:

(1) name of agency
(2) address of agency
(3) phone number of agency
(4) name of contact person at agency
(5) office hours
(6) cost of service/financial assistance available
(7) services offered
(8) eligibility requirements
(9) how to apply for services
(10) other information about services
(11) layout of offices
(12) brochures and other relevant printed materials explaining services of each agency to give to group members

A caregiver may wish to summarize the above information for each agency and develop an Agency Information Sheet. A copy of the Agency Information Sheet is located in Appendix B.

If a caregiver does not have time to visit each agency, it is suggested that he or she obtain this information by telephone. The agency may be willing to send brochures and other printed materials by mail in response to a telephone inquiry.

A caregiver may wish to invite several service providers and/or family members utilizing these services to meet as a group. Service providers from agencies that are most likely to be utilized should be considered. These persons could

—provide specific input about their services,
—give a service provider's perspective of what it is like to relate to families,
—give a family member's perspective of what it is like to relate to community resources,
—and answer group members' questions.

The following is a listing of services and agencies (adopted from Goodman, 1980) a caregiver may wish to contact for material. This listing is not mutually exclusive or exhaustive. One agency may offer several of these services. A caregiver may be aware of other relevant services available in a geographic area that should be contacted.

Social Security Office
    Social Security Benefits
    Medicare
    Medicaid
Public Welfare Office
    Food Stamps
    SSI—Supplemental Security Income
Meals-on-Wheels Programs that may be offered through churches or synagogues, hospitals, nursing homes, or community centers
Area Agency on Aging
Country Council on Aging
Homemaker services available through family service agencies and private organizations
Home-health aid programs
Public Health Department—visiting nurses
Services to the Blind
Internal Revenue Services for tax relief for elderly home owners and renters
Crime prevention programs
Adult day care programs
Friendly visiting programs
Telephone reassurance programs
Counseling services/community mental health center
Low-cost drugs for older adults
Information and referral services
Free medical screening tests
Recreation programs

Local nursing homes

Local retirement facilities

Special services of the cancer, heart, and diabetes associations

Transportation services for older adults

Glaucoma clinics

Shopping assistance

Legal services

Protective services

Local hospitals—highlight services often utilized by older adults, such as stroke rehabilitation team, physical therapy

Local weatherization programs

Assistance with utility bills

Escort services

Handyman services

Low-income housing

Other respite care programs

Support programs

Self-help groups

SUMMARY

Formal support systems provide services that can supplement the caregiving provided by family and friends. It is important *to match the needs of the caregiver and older person's with the services provided by the formal systems.* In all instances, *the objective should be to maximize the independence of the older person and minimize the stress of the primary caregiver.* Many times the match of formal and informal support systems will achieve this objective. For example, an older person's independence may be maximized when an agency provides respite care for an older person. At the same time, the caregiver's level of stress is reduced because he or she has an opportunity to be relieved of the caregiving responsibilities.

The key is the matching of the formal and informal support systems. To enhance this process, it is important for the caregiver and older person to know his or her needs as well as the available assistance from formal and informal support systems. The Action Plan presented in Chapter 9 provides a way to develop knowledge of these factors so that caregivers can create a match in their particular situation.

SUGGESTIONS FOR PRACTICE

1. Form a group of caregivers and have them discuss their feelings when they work with service providers. Discuss these feelings in terms of the caregivers' frustrations with the caregiving situation and the manner in which the providers dealt with them. Did they feel that the service providers understood their situations? Did the caregivers perceive the limitations the providers had in delivering the services?

2. Establish a Service Fair in the community. Invite representatives from various service agencies to display their services. Publicize the fair in the newspaper and on the radio so that families are encouraged to come and learn abut the various services available within the community.

3. Encourage caregivers to use the Agency Information Sheet to create an awareness of the services available in the community. The providers may want to use these forms to visit the Service Fair noted above. It might be helpful to hold a group meeting of caregivers so they can share the information from the Agency Information Sheet with one another.

RESOURCE LIST

In order to obtain additional information about formal support systems, you may want to explore the following resources:

Books

Harbert, A. S., & Ginsberg, L. H. (1979). *Human services for older adults: Concept and skills.* Belmont, CA: Wadsworth.
Horn, L., & Griesel, E. (1977). *Nursing home: A citizens' action guide.* 25 Beaon Street, Boston, MA 02108.
Kerr, J. O., & Whitney, S. E. (1981). *Community intervention for the elderly: A catalog of innovative and effective programs,* Portland: Institute on Aging, Portland State University.
Ragan, P. K. (Ed.). (1979). *Aging parents.* Los Angeles: University of Southern California Press.
Silverman, P. R. (1980). *Mutual help groups: Organization and development.* Beverly Hills, CA: Sage.

Chapter 9

ACTION PLAN AND
CAREGIVER KNOWLEDGE EXERCISE

Two activities designed for caregivers are included in this chapter. The first is an Action Plan that has been developed to encourage caregivers to examine their needs and the resources available within the informal and formal support systems. Guidelines for completing an Action Plan and a sample plan are included. An incomplete Action Plan is included in Appendix B. Caregivers are encouraged to remove the Action Plan form from Appendix B and use it to help them in their caregiving situation.

The second activity is a Caregiver Knowledge Excercise. This excercise includes two parts. Part I focuses on knowledge about older people and aspects of caregiving. There are 25 true/false statements based on the content of Chapters 1-8. The correct answers are listed in Appendix A. Part II presents questions that help a caregiver to examine his or her caregiving situation closely. The answers are related to the position or situation of each caregiver.

It is our hope that these activities will help caregivers apply the contents of this book to their unique situation, and that they will be able to maximize the independence of the older person and minimize the stress they may feel.

GUIDELINES FOR COMPLETION OF THE ACTION PLAN

In this book we have discussed some of the stress-producing situations a caregiver might experience. We have also discussed the importance of receiving support from family members, friends, neighbors, and community services in order to lessen some of the stresses caregivers experience. The Action Plan is designed to provide the opportunity for caregivers to consider any informal and/or formal supports that might assist with these needs. The Action Plan is presented in Appendix A.

This Action Plan is for caregivers and their older family members. You do not need to show it to anyone. However, you may wish to receive feedback from other caregivers about your plans. Once you have had time to initiate some of your plans, you may wish to share how satisfactory they are with other caregivers and/or family members. You may want to ask others to help you make adjustments on your action plan.

There are no right or wrong action plans. A plan that may be exactly right for you may be exactly wrong for someone else. However, for the plan to be useful, it is necessary to describe specifically what your needs are and to be realistic about the kinds of supports that may meet some of these needs.

This Action Plan is not set in stone. What appears to be an appropriate plan one day may need to be adjusted later as changes take place in an older family member's and/or your health, in your life situations, or in the services offered by community resources.

As you complete the Action Plan, caregivers may feel excited about discovering new people and services to assist with the caregiving responsibilities. For some, this excitement may turn to discouragement, anger, and/or feelings of loneliness if a person or service from whom you request assistance cannot be involved. Others may feel pain and isolation because of a new awareness that there is no satisfactory solution to the situation—your decisions may not be about what the really good alternatives are, but rather about what the least harmful alternative is. Those decisions can be painful. Our hope is that you will have developed enough rapport with another caregiver that if you experience feelings of anger, frustration, or loneliness you will share those with the other caregiver. Be sure to share your joys too! Remember, caregivers need to support one another.

DIRECTIONS FOR COMPLETING THE ACTION PLAN

(1) The Action II Plan is given in a booklet format. On the first page of the booklet, write your name, the date, and *one* need you are experiencing

with your caregiving responsibilities. Only *one* need should be dealt with in each booklet. If you have five needs you want assistance with, you will complete five booklets. You may want to consider your physical, social, emotional, and economic needs as you complete this exercise.

(2) In Column 1 (INFORMAL SUPPORTS) list any family members, friends or neighbors you think can assist you with the need identified on page 1. Refer to the example given.

(3) In Column 2 (HOW MIGHT HE/SHE ASSIST?) list specific ways you think the person listed in the corresponding INFORMAL SUPPORTS column can help meet the need being addressed. Refer to the example given.

(4) In Column 3 (ADVANTAGES OF HIS/HER ASSISTANCE), identify any pluses or benefits you may experience through receiving assistance from the persons listed in Column 1. Refer to the example.

(5) In Column 4 (DISADVANTAGES OF HIS/HER ASSISTANCE) identify any obstacles or minuses you may encounter in receiving assistance from the persons listed in Column 1. Refer to example.

(6) In Column 5 (POSSIBLE WAYS TO OVERCOME DISADVANTAGES) list any ways the obstacles in Column 4 may be lessened or overcome. See the example.

(7) After carefully considering the information in Columns 1-5, identify in Column 6 (ACTIONS I WILL TAKE) the specific thing(s) you want to do in order to try to lessen your need as identified on page 1. See example.

(8) In Column 7 (WHEN) identfy the time period in which you plan to carry out each action listed in Column 6. See example.

(9) In Column 8 (FORMAL SUPPORTS) list any community services or agencies you think can assist you with your need. Refer to the example given.

(10) In Column 9 (WHAT SERVICES MIGHT BE USED) list any specific ways you think the agency can assist you with this need. See example.

(11) In Column 10 (ADVANTAGES OF USING THE SERVICE) identify any "pluses" or benefits you may experience through receiving assistance from the agencies listed in Column 8. Refer to the example.

(12) In Column 11 (DISADVANTAGES OF USING THE SERVICE) identify any obstacles or "minuses" you may encounter in receiving assistance from the agencies listed in Column 8. See example.

(13) In Column 12 (POSSIBLE WAYS TO OVERCOME DISADVANTAGES) identify any ways the obstacles in Column 11 may be overcome. See example.

(14) After carefully considering the information in Columns 8-12, identify in Column 13 (ACTION/S I WILL TAKE) the specific thing(s) you want to do in order to try to lessen your need as identified on page 1. See example.

(15) In Column 14 (WHEN) identify the time period in which you plan to carry out each action listed in Column 13. See example.

Activity

EXAMPLE: You may wish to show this example to your group members to give them an idea of how to complete their Action Plan.

ACTION PLAN

NAME:___Jane Doe_____

DATE:___5/25/84_____

NEED:____I feel so isolated. I need more time to_____

_____spend with friends._____

_____

-2-

HOW MIGHT HE/SHE ASSIST?

1. stay with Mom one afternoon a week

2. stop by for coffee Tuesday a.m.

3. _____

4. _____

5. _____

-4-

DISADVANTAGES OF HIS/HER ASSISTANCE

1. she doesn't have transportation

2. none

3. _____

4. _____

5. _____

-1-

INFORMAL SUPPORTS
(family, friends, neighbors)

1. Aunt Mary

2. Sally

3. _____

4. _____

5. _____

-3-

ADVANTAGES OF HIS/HER ASSISTANCE

1. Mary wants to spend time w/Mom

2. Sally's a great friend! Life seems more hopeful after I talk w/her.

3. _____

4. _____

5. _____

-5-

POSSIBLE WAYS TO OVERCOME
DISADVANTAGES

1. Mary's daughter can bring her

2. —

3. _____

4. _____

5. _____

-6-

ACTION(S) I WILL TAKE

1. Invite Sally to come regularly for coffee

2. Talk with Aunt Mary about coming by regularly

3. _____

4. _____

5. _____

-7-

WHEN

1. call Sally on Friday

2. call tomorrow afternoon

3. _____

4. _____

5. _____

WHAT SERVICES MIGHT BE USED?

1. ask for friendly visitor for Mom

2. have Mom spend 1 –2 days/week there

3. _____

4. _____

5. _____

FORMAL SUPPORTS
(community services)

1. Council on Aging—Friendly Visitor

2. Adult Day Care Center

3. _____

4. _____

5. _____

DISADVANTAGES OF USING
THE SERVICE

1. none

2. Mom afraid to go to Center

3. _____

4. _____

5. _____

ADVANTAGES OF USING
THE SERVICE

1. Agency has good reputation; know I can trust anyone they send.

2. Know they have good services; Mom could meet new friends.

3. _____

4. _____

5. _____

ACTION(S) I WILL TAKE

1. check out Adult Day Care Center
2. _____
3. _____
4. _____
5. _____

POSSIBLE WAYS TO OVERCOME
DISADVANTAGES

1. —
2. Contact center. Maybe Director could stop by several times to learn to know Mom and reassure her that she would be safe; go with Mom first several times to Center.
3. _____
4. _____
5. _____

WHEN

1. Call Director tomorrow a.m. to arrange an appt.
2. _____
3. _____
4. _____
5. _____

Activity II
Caregiver's Knowledge Exercise

PART I

Circle the answer

T	F	1. Senile dementia is a normal age-related change.
T	F	2. A person's environment and lifestyle do not affect the speed of his/her aging process.
T	F	3. Some age-related changes occur in some people but not in others.
T	F	4. The majority of persons 65 and over do not have adequate health to live independently.
T	F	5. Even though there are physical changes accompanying old age, most older people are able to cope well because the changes are gradual enough that they are able to make the necessary psychological and emotional adjustments.
T	F	6. Caregiving stresses are interrelated. The effects of one stress may directly or indirectly influence *all* of the caregiver's functioning.
T	F	7. The stresses of caregiving seldom cause increased health problems for the caregiver.
T	F	8. It is usually best to make decisions for older dependent family members without consulting them.
T	F	9. When an older person becomes frail, his/her child can best help by reversing roles with the parent. The child assumes the parent role and the parent becomes the child.
T	F	10. A caregiver's feelings about his/her own aging do not determine the quality of care he/she gives to the older dependent family member.
T	F	11. Even though a caregiver may resent having to take care of an older family member, he/she can usually hide those feelings from the older relative if he/she tries hard enough.
T	F	12. A good relationship between an older family member and his/her caregiver can become even closer if healthy patterns of relating together are continued.
T	F	13. A caregiver should not try to find time for himself/herself if the older family member seems to need constant attention.
T	F	14. It is common for caregivers to feel guilty during their caregiving experiences.
T	F	15. A person may age more rapidly if he/she does not have opportunities to communicate with others.

T   F   16. Older dependent family members will feel more secure and happier if other family members take complete control of their lives.

T   F   17. Each family has its own language.

T   F   18. When a stroke victim cannot speak, this is usually an indication that he/she also cannot understand what others say to him/her.

T   F   19. It is sometimes difficult to communicate with community service agencies because each agency tends to develop its own language and communication systems.

T   F   20. A person involved in caregiving runs a higher risk of illness unless he/she has a planned support system to fill the gaps.

T   F   21. Continued friendships seem to promote higher morale among persons than do ongoing family relationships.

T   F   22. A caregiver can give ongoing support to his/her old family member even if he/she does not receive any support.

T   F   23. Sometimes it is more helpful to receive assistance from community agencies than it is from family, friends, or neighbors.

T   F   24. Family members can assume all needed caregiving responsibilities.

T   F   25. Caregivers sometimes feel guilty about transferring certain caregiving responsibilities to agency personnel.

PART II

Section I

1. Are *you* receiving emotional support (visits, telephone calls, opportunities to express your feelings about caregiving, etc.) from other family members, friends, and/or neighbors?

_____ yes   _____ no

a. If yes, what is their relationship to you? (please check all that apply)

_____ sister   _____ friend

_____ brother   _____ neighbor

_____ cousin   _____ someone from your church

_____ aunt   _____ other (please specify)

_____ uncle   _____

_____ child(ren)   _____

_____ grandchild(ren)

b. Approximately how many contacts do you have each week with family members, friends, or neighbors?

_____ 0   _____ 5–6
_____ 1–2   _____ 7–10
_____ 3–4   _____ more than 10; how many? _____

2. Would you like your *family members* to give you emotional support as you are caring for your older family member?

_____ yes   _____ no

a. If no, why not? _____
_____

3. Would you like your *friends* to give you emotional support as you are caring for your older family members?

_____ yes   _____ no

a. If no, why not? _____
_____

4. Would you like your *neighbors* to give you emotional support as you are caring for your older family member?

_____ yes   _____ no

a. If no, why not? _____
_____

5. Would you like people from your church to give you emotional support as you are caring for your older family member?

_____ yes   _____ no

a. If no, why not? _____
_____

6. Do you feel free to ask for emotional support from:
   a. family members?   _____ yes   _____ no
   b. friends?   _____ yes   _____ no
   c. neighbors?   _____ yes   _____ no
   d. someone from your church?   _____ yes   _____ no
   e. If no, why not? _____
   _____

7. Are you receiving enough emotional support from family members, friends, neighbors, and church members?

_____ yes   _____ no

a. If no, from whom would you like to receive more emotional support?
_____ family members   _____ neighbors
_____ friends   _____ people from your church
   b. What kind of additional emotional support would you like?
_____
_____
_____

Section II

1. Do you receive any kind of assistance from:
   a. family members?   _____ yes   _____ no
   b. friends?   _____ yes   _____ no
   c. neighbors?   _____ yes   _____ no
   d. people from your church?   _____ yes   _____ no
   e. If yes, what kind? (please place an **a** in all categories that family members assist you with; **b** for friends; **c** for neighbors, and **d** for persons from your church).

   _____ cleaning   _____ provide companionship
   _____ cooking   to dependent elderly
   _____ laundry   family member
   _____ car maintenance   _____ provide emotional
   _____ maintenance on house   support (good listener,
   _____ yardwork   offer helpful
   _____ gardening   suggestions)
   _____ financial   _____ shopping
   _____ physical care of   _____ banking
             dependent family   _____ see that bills are paid
             member   _____ stay with older relative
   _____ provide companionship   so you can leave home
             to you   for awhile
   _____ other (please specify) _____

2. Do you feel free to ask for assistance from:
   a. family members?   _____ yes   _____ no
   b. friends?   _____ yes   _____ no
   c. neighbors?   _____ yes   _____ no
   d. people from your church?   _____ yes   _____ no
   e. If no, why not? _____

3. Are you receiving enough assistance from family members, friends, and/or neighbors?
                     _____ yes   _____ no
   a. If no, from whom would you like more assistance?
      _____ family members   _____ neighbors
      _____ friends   _____ people from church

4. What additional assistance would you like? _____
   _____

Section III

1. Do you receive assistance in the care of your dependent family member from any social service agency or other formal organization?
                     _____ yes   _____ no

a. If yes, which one(s)? (please check all that apply)

_____ Home Health Agency   _____ Self-Help Group

_____ Mental Health Center   _____ Meals on Wheels

_____ Public Health Dept.   _____ Adult Day Care

_____ Homemaker Service   Program

_____ Social Security   _____ Information and

_____ Respite Care Program   Referral Services

_____ Support Group   _____ Council on Aging

_____ Supplementary   _____ Medicaid

     Security Income   _____ Medicare

_____ Other (please specify) _____

b. Approximately how often does someone from a social service agency or formal organization assist you?

_____ less than once a month   _____ 3–5 times per week

_____ once a month   _____ 6–9 times per week

_____ 2–3 times per month   _____ 10 times per week

_____ 1–2 times per week   or more

c. What kind of assistance do you receive from social service agencies or other formal organizations?

_____ cleaning   _____ provide companionship

_____ cooking   to dependent elderly

_____ laundry   family member

_____ car maintenance   _____ provide emotional

_____ maintenance on house   support (good listener;

_____ yardwork   offer helpful

_____ gardening   suggestions)

_____ financial   _____ shopping

_____ physical care of   _____ banking

     dependent family   _____ see that bills are paid

     member   _____ stay with dependent

_____ provide companionship   family member so that

     to you   you can leave your

          home for awhile

_____ other (please specify) _____

2. Do you feel free to ask for assistance from formal service agencies?

_____ yes   _____ no

a. If no, why not? _____

_____

3. Are you receiving enough assistance from formal service agencies?

_____ yes   _____ no

a. If no, from which agencies would you like additional assistance?

_____

_____

4. What additional assistance would you like? _____
_____

Thank you for completing this exercise.

SUGGESTIONS FOR PRACTICE

1. In a group or individual setting, encourage caregivers to complete the Action Plan. Discuss the plan with them and urge them to display it in a prominent place within their homes. Urge them to note when they have taken the action to receive assistance.

2. If a seminar, workshop, or other educational program was developed around this book, urge the caregivers to complete the Caregiver Knowledge Exercise. Discuss the answers and encourage the caregivers to apply the material to their caregiving situations.

APPENDIX A:
Answers to the Caregiver's Knowledge Exercise (Part I)

Question Number	Answer	Discussion Found in Chapter
1	False	Chapter 2
2	False	Chapter 2
3	True	Chapter 2
4	False	Chapter 2
5	True	Chapter 2
6	True	Chapter 3
7	False	Chapter 3
8	False	Chapter 3
9	False	Chapter 3
10	False	Chapter 3
11	False	Chapter 4
12	True	Chapter 4
13	False	Chapters 3, 4, 7, 8
14	True	Chapter 4
15	True	Chapter 5
16	False	Chapter 6
17	True	Chapter 6
18	False	Chapter 6
19	True	Chapter 6
20	True	Chapter 7
21	True	Chapter 7
22	False	Chapter 7, 8
23	True	Chapter 8
24	False	Chapters 7, 8
25	True	Chapter 8

APPENDIX B:
Agency Information Sheet

AGENCY INFORMATION SHEET

Agency Name: _____
Address: _____
Phone Number: _____
Contact Person: _____
Office Hours: _____
Cost of Services/Financial
    Assistance Available: _____
Transportation Available to
    Services: _____
Services Offered: _____

Eligibility Requirements: _____

How to Apply for Services: _____

Other Information about Services: _____

Layout of Offices (note obstructions to
    physically handicapped persons): _____

AGENCY INFORMATION SHEET

Agency Name: _____
Address: _____
Phone Number: _____
Contact Person: _____
Office Hours: _____
Cost of Services/Financial
    Assistance Available: _____
Transportation Available to
    Services: _____
Services Offered: _____

Eligibility Requirements: _____

How to Apply for Services: _____

Other Information about Services: _____

Layout of Offices (note obstructions to
    physically handicapped persons): _____

145

APPENDIX C:
ACTION PLAN

ACTION PLAN

NAME: _____

DATE: _____

NEED: _____
_____
_____

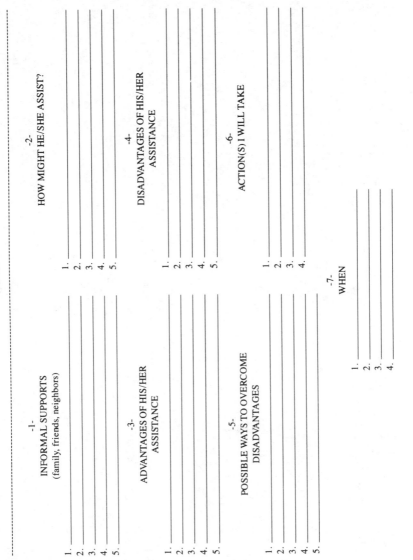

-1-
INFORMAL SUPPORTS
(family, friends, neighbors)

1. _____
2. _____
3. _____
4. _____
5. _____

-2-
HOW MIGHT HE/SHE ASSIST?

1. _____
2. _____
3. _____
4. _____
5. _____

-3-
ADVANTAGES OF HIS/HER
ASSISTANCE

1. _____
2. _____
3. _____
4. _____
5. _____

-4-
DISADVANTAGES OF HIS/HER
ASSISTANCE

1. _____
2. _____
3. _____
4. _____
5. _____

-5-
POSSIBLE WAYS TO OVERCOME
DISADVANTAGES

1. _____
2. _____
3. _____
4. _____
5. _____

-6-
ACTION(S) I WILL TAKE

1. _____
2. _____
3. _____
4. _____

-7-
WHEN

1. _____
2. _____
3. _____
4. _____

Tear out

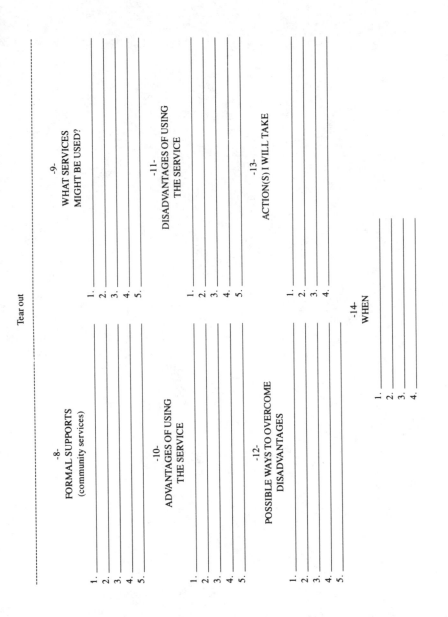

-8-
FORMAL SUPPORTS
(community services)

1.
2.
3.
4.
5.

-9-
WHAT SERVICES
MIGHT BE USED?

1.
2.
3.
4.
5.

-10-
ADVANTAGES OF USING
THE SERVICE

1.
2.
3.
4.
5.

-11-
DISADVANTAGES OF USING
THE SERVICE

1.
2.
3.
4.
5.

-12-
POSSIBLE WAYS TO OVERCOME
DISADVANTAGES

1.
2.
3.
4.
5.

-13-
ACTION(S) I WILL TAKE

1.
2.
3.
4.

-14-
WHEN

1.
2.
3.
4.

REFERENCES

ARCHBOLD, P. G. (1980) "Impact of parent caring on middle-aged offspring." Journal of Gerontological Nursing 6: 79-85.

ATCHLEY, R. C. (1983) Aging: Continuity and Change. Belmont, CA: Wadsworth.

_____ (1980) The Social Forces in Later Life (3rd ed.). Belmont, CA: Wadsworth.

_____ and S. J. MILLER (1980) "Older people and their families," in C. Eisendorfer (ed.) Annual Review of Gerontology and Geriatrics. New York: Springer.

BACK, K. W. (1977) "Social systems and social facts," in E. Shanas and M. B. Sussman (eds.) Family, Bureaucracy and the Elderly. Durham, NC: Duke University Press.

BARRESI, C. M. and T. H. BRUBAKER (1979) "Clinical social workers' knowledge about aging: responses to the "Facts on Aging' quiz." Journal of Gerontological Social Work 2: 137-146.

BELL, W. G. (1973) "Community care for the elderly: an alternative to institutionalization." The Gerontologist 13: 349-354

BETTINGHAUS, C. O. and E. P. BETTINGHAUS (1976) "Communication considerations in the health care of the aging," in H. J. Oyer and E. J. Oyer (eds.) Aging and Communication Baltimore: University Park Press.

BLAZER, D. (1978) "Working with the elderly patient's family." Geriatrics 33: 117-118, 123.

BLENKNER, M. (1965) "Social work and family relationships in later life with some thoughts on filial maturity," in E. Shanas and G. F. Streib (eds.) Social Structure and the Family Englewood Cliffs,NJ: Prentice-Hall.

BRANCH, L. G. and A. JETTE (1983) "Elder's use of informal long-term care assistance." The Gerontologist 23: 51-56.

BRANDWEIN, C. A. and R. POSTOFF (1980) "A model of intervention for working with adult children of aged parents." Long Term Care and Health Services Administration 4: 173-182.

BRILL, N. I. (1973) Working with People—The Helping Process. New York: J. B. Lippincott.

BRODY, E. M. (1981) "'Women in the middle' and family help to older people." The Gerontologist 21: 471-480.

_____ (1979) "Aging parents and aging children," in P. K. Ragan (ed.) Aging Parents. Los Angeles: University of Southern California Press.

_____ (1978) "The aging family." Annuals of the American Academy of Political and Social Science 438: 13-27.

_____ (1977) Long-Term Care of Older People: A Practical Guide New York: Human Sciences Press.

BRODY, S. J., W. POULSHOCK, and C. F. MASCIOCCHI (1978) "The family caring unit: a major consideration in the long-term support system." The Gerontologist 18: 556-561.

BRUBAKER, T. H. (ed.) (1983) Family Relationships in Later Life. Beverly Hills, CA: Sage.

———— and C. M. BARRESI (1979) "Social workers' levels of knowledge about old age and perceptions of service delivery to the elderly." Research on Aging 1: 213-233.

———— and E. BRUBAKER (1981) "Adult children and elderly parent household." Alternative Lifestyles 4: 242-256.

———— and C. B. HENNON (1982) "Responsibility for household tasks: comparing dual earner and dual retired marriages," in M. Szinovacz (ed.) Women's Retirement Beverly Hills, CA: Sage.

———— and E. A. POWERS (1976) "The stereotype of 'old': a review and alternative approach." Journal of Gerontology 31: 441-447.

BURNAGIN, V. E. and K. P. HIRN (1979) Aging is a Family Affair. New York: J. B. Lippincott.

BUTLER, R. N. (1975) Why Survive?: Being Old in America. New York: Harper & Row.

———— (1968) "The life review: an interpretation of reminiscence in the aged,;; in B. L. Neugarten (ed.) Middle Age and Aging. Chicago: University of Chicago Press.

———— and M. LEWIS (1977) Aging and Mental Health (2nd ed.). St. Louis: C. V. Mosby.

CANTOR, M. J. (1983) "Strain among Caregivers: a study of experience in the United States." The Gerontologist 23: 597-610.

———— (1979) "Neighbors and Friends: an overlooked resource in the informal support system." Research on Aging 1: 434-463.

CAPLAN, G. (1974) Support Systems and Community Mental Health. New York: Behavioral Publications.

CHEN, P. N., S. L. BELL, D. L. DOLINSKY, J. DOYLE, and M. DUNN (1981) "Elderly abuse in domestic settings: a pilot study." Journal of Gerontological Social Work 4: 3-17.

CICIRELLI, V. G. (1981) Helping Elderly Parents: The Role of Adult Children. Boston: Auburn House.

COHEN, S. Z. and B. M. GANS (1978) The Other Generation Gap. Chicago: Follett.

COMBS, A. W., D. AVILA, and W. W. PURKEY (1971) Helping Relationships: Basic Concepts for the Helping Professions. Boston: Allyn & Bacon.

CROSSMAN, L., C. LONDON, and C. BARRY (1981) "Older women caring for disabled spouses: a model for supportive services." The Gerontologist 21: 464-470.

CURTIN, S. R. (1972) Nobody Ever Died of Old Age Boston: Little, Brown.

EGAN, G. (1976) Interpersonal Living. Monterey, CA: Brooks/Cole.

ERIKSEN, K. (1979) Communications Skills for the Human Services. Reston, VA: Reston Publishing.

ERNST, M., and H. SHORE (1975) Sensitizing People to the Processes of Aging: The In-Service Educator's Guide. Denton: Center for Studies in Aging, North Texas State University.

EVANS, D. R., M. T. HEARN, M. R. UHLEMAN, and A. E. IVEY (1979) Essential Interviewing. Monterey, CA: Brooks/Cole.

FENGLER, A. P. and N. GOODRICH (1979) "Wives of elderly disabled men: the hidden patients." The Gerontologist 19: 175-183.

FRANKFATHER, D. L., M. J. SMITH, and F. G. CARO (1981) Family Care of the Elderly. Lexington, MA: D. C. Heath.

GALVIN, K. M. and B. J. BROMMEL (1982) Family Communication: Cohesion and Change. Glenview, IL: Scott, Foresman.

The Gerontologist (1983) "Symposium: aging and the family; informal support systems." Vol. 32.

GETZEL, G. S. (1981) "Social work with family caregivers." Social Casework 61: 201-209.

GILBERT, J. G. (1977) Paraprofessionals and the Elderly. Greenville, NY: Panel Publishers.

GILES, J. (1981) A Guide to Caring for and Coping with Aging Parents. Nashville, TN: Thomas Nelson.

GOODMAN, J. G. (1980) Aging Parents: Whose Responsibility? New York: Family Service Association of America.

GREENBERG, L., B. FATULA, D. R. HAMEISTER, and T. HICKEY (1976) Communication Skills for the Gerontological Practitioner. University Park: The Gerontology Center, Pennsylvania State University.

GWYTHER, L. (1982) "Caring for caregivers: a statewide family support program mobilizes mutual help." Center Reports on Advances in Research 6: 1-7. Durham, NC: Duke University Center for the Study of Aging and Human Development.

HAMRICK, K. and D. BLAZER (1980) "Older adults and their families in a community mental health center: strategies for intervention." Hospital and Community Psychiatry 31: 332-335.

HARBERT, A. S. and L. H. GINSBERG (1979) Human Services for Older Adults: Concepts and Skills. Belmont, CA: Wadsworth.

HARTFORD, M. E. and R. PARSONS (1982) "Groups with relatives of dependent older adults." The Gerontologist 22: 394-398.

HAUSMAN, C. P. (1979) "Short-term counseling groups for people with elderly parents." The Gerontologist 19: 102-107.

HERR, J. J. and J. H. WEAKLAND (1979) Counseling Elders and Their Familes. New York: Springer.

HICKEY, T. and R. L. DOUGLAS (1981) "Neglect and abuse of older family members: Professionals' perspective and case experiences." The Gerontologist 21: 610-618.

———— and B. FATULA (1978) Sensory Deprivation and the Elderly: Gerontology Practitioner Training Manual. University Park: The Gerontology Center, Pennsylvania State University.

HORN, L. and E. GRIESEL (1977) Nursing Homes: A Citizens' Action Guide. 25 Beacon Street, Boston, MA.

JOHNSON, C. L. and D. J. CATALANO (1981) "Childless elderly and their family supports." The Gerontologist 21: 610-618.

JOHNSON, D. W. (1972) Reaching Out: Interpersonal Effectiveness and Self-Actualization. Englewood Cliffs, NJ: Prentice-Hall.

JOHNSON, E. S. and B. J. BURSK (1977) "Relationships between the elderly and their adult children." The Gerontologist 17: 90-96.

KEITH, P. M. and T. H. BRUBAKER (1979) "Male household roles in later life: a look at masculinity and marital relationships." The Family Coordinator 29: 497-502.

KERR, J. O. and S. E. WHITNEY (1981) Community Intervention for the Elderly: A Catalog of Innovative and Effective Programs. Portland: OR. Institute on Aging, Portland State University.

KUMIN, L. (1978) Aphasia. Lincoln, NE: Cliff Notes.

LEBOWITZ, B. (1978) "Old age and family functioning." Journal of Gerontological Social Work 1: 111-118.

L'ENGLE, M. (1979) The Summer of the Great Grandmother. New York: Seabury Press.

LEWIS, M. I. and R. M. BUTLER (1977) "Life review therapy." Geriatrics 29: 165-173.

LITWAK, E. and I. SZELENYI (1969) "Primary group structures and their functions: kin, neighbors and friends." American Sociological Review 34: 465-481.

Loss Reaction and Grief Management (1976) University Park: The Gerontology Center, Pennsylvania State University.

MACE, N. L. and P. V. RABINS (1981) The 36-Hour Day: A Family Guide to Caring for Persons with Alzheimer's Disease, Related Dementing Illnesses and Memory Loss in Later Life. Baltimore: Johns Hopkins University Press.

MACLAY, E. (1977) Green Winter: Celebrations of Old Age. New York: McGraw-Hill.

McCUBBIN, H. I., C. B. JOY, A. E. CAUBLE, J. K. COMEAU, J. M. PATTERSON, and R. H. NEEDLE (1980) "Family stress and coping: a decade review." Journal of Marriage and the Family 42: 855-867.

McGREEHAN, D. M. and S. W. WARBURTON (1978) "How to help families cope with caring for elderly members." Geriatrics 33: 99-106.

MILLAR, D. P. and F. E. MILLAR (1976) Messages and Myths. Washington, NY: Alfred.

MILLER, D. A. (1981) "The sandwich generation: adult children of the aging." Social Work 26: 419-423.

MORONEY, R. M. (1976) The Family and the State: Considerations for Social Policy. New York: Longman.

MUNNICHS, J. M. A. (1977) "Linkages of old people with their families and bureaucracy in a welfare state, The Netherlands," in E. Shanas and M. B. Sussman (eds.) Family, Bureaucracy and the Elderly. Durham, NC: Duke University Press.

NEUHAUS, R. and R. NEUHAUS (1982) Successful Aging. New York: John Wiley.

OKUN, B. F. (1980) Effective Helping (2nd ed.). Monterey, CA: Brooks/Cole.

OTTEN, J. and F. SHELLY (1976) When Your Parents Grow Old. New York: Funk and Wagnells.

OYER, E. J. (1976) "Exchanging information within the older family," in H. J. Oyer and E. J. Oyer (eds.) Aging and Communication. Baltimore: University Park Press.

OYER, H. J. and E. J. OYER (1976) "Communicating with older people: basic considerations," in H. J. Oyer and E. J. Oyer (eds.) Aging and Communication. Baltimore: University Park Press.

PALMORE, E. (1976) "Total chance of institutionalization among the aged." The Gerontologist 16: 504-507.

PETTY, B. J., T. P. MOELLER, and R. Z. CAMPBELL (1976) "Support groups for elderly persons in the community." The Gerontologist 15: 522-528.

RAGAN, P. K. [ed.] (1979) Aging Parents. Los Angeles: University of Southern California Press.

RAKOWSKI, W. and T. HICKEY (1976) Basic Concepts in Aging. University Park: The Gerontology Center, Pennsylvania State University.

RATHBONE-McCUAN, E. (1976) "Geriatric day care: a family perspective." The Gerontologist 16: 517-521.

REUBEN, S. and G. K. BYRNES (1977) "Helping elderly patients in the transition to a nursing home." Geriatrics 32: 107-108, 110, 112.

ROBINSON, B. and M. THURNER (1979) "Taking care of aged parents: a family cycle tradition." The Gerontologist 19: 586-593.

ROCKSTEIN, M. and M. SUSSMAN (1979) Biology of Aging. Belmont, CA: Wadsworth.

ROLL, S. O. T. R./L., M. G. S. (1981) Personal interview.

SAFFORD, F. (1980) "A program for families of the mentally impaired elderly." The Gerontologist 20: 656-660.

SCHMIDT, M. G. (1981) "Personal networks: assessment, care and repair." Journal of Gerontological Social Work 3: 65-70.

———— (1980) "Failing parents, aging children." Journal of Gerontological Social Work 2: 259-268.

SCHWARTZ, A. N. (1977) Survival Handbook for Children of Aging Parents. Chicago: Follett.

SCORESBY, A. L. (1977) The Marriage Dialogue. Reading, MA: Addison-Wesley.

SEDGWICK, R. (1981) Family Mental Health: Theory and Practice. St. Louis: C. V. Mosby.

Self-Maintenance Skills (1976) University Park: The Gerontology Center, Pennsylvania State University.

SHANAS, E. (1979a) "The family as a social support system in old age." The Gerontologist 19: 169-174.

———— (1979b) "Social myth as hypothesis: the case of the family relations of old people." The Gerontologist 19: 3-9.

———— and M. SUSSMAN [eds.] (1977) Family, Bureaucracy, and The Elderly. Durham, NC: Duke University Press.

SILVERMAN, A. G. and C. I. BRAHCE (1979) "'As parents grow older': an intervention model." Journal of Gerontological Social Work 2: 77-83.

SILVERMAN, A. G., B. KAHN, and G. ANDERSON (1977) "A model for working with multi-generational families." Social Casework 58: 131-135.

SILVERMAN, P. R. (1980) Mutual Help Groups: Organization and Development. Beverly Hills, CA: Sage.

SILVERSTONE, B. and H. H. HYMAN (1982) You and Your aging Parent (rev. ed.). New York: Pantheon.

SINE, R. D. [ed.] (1977) Basic Rehabilitation Techniques: A Self-Instructional Guide. Germantown, NY: Aspen.

SOLDO, B. J. and J. MYLLYLUOMA (1983) "Caregivers who live with dependent elderly." The Gerontologist 23: 605-611.

STEINITZ, D. Y. (1981) "The local church as support for the elderly." Journal of Gerontological Social Work 4: 43-53.

STEINMETZ, S. K. and D. J. AMSDEN (1983) "Dependent elders, family stress and abuse," in T. H. Brubaker (ed.) Family Relationships in Later Life. Beverly Hills, CA: Sage.

TAMIR, L. M. (1979) Communications and the Aging Process. New York: Pergamon.

TOBIN, S. S. and R. KULYS (1980) "Family and service," in C. Eisdorfer (ed.) Annual Review of Gerontology and Geriatrics. New York: Springer.

TOWNSEND, P. (1965) "The effects of family structure on the likelihood of admission to an institution in old age," in E. Shanas and G. F. Streib (eds.) Social Structure and the Family: Generational Relations. Englewood Cliffs, NJ: Prentice-Hall.

TROLL, L. E., S. J. MILLER, and R. C. ATCHLEY (1979) Families in Later Life. Belmont, CA: Wadsworth.

VINING, E. G. (1978) Being Seventy: The measure of a Year. New York: Viking.

WARD, R. A. (1978) "Limitations of the family as a supportive institution in the lives of the aged." The Family Coordinator 27: 365-371.

WATERS, E., A. WEAVER, and B. WHITE (1980) Gerontological Counseling Skills: A Manual for Training Service Providers. Rochester, MI: Continuum Center for Adult Counseling and Leadership Training, Oakland University.

WEIHAUS, S. (1979) "Aging is a family affair," in P. K. Ragan (ed.) Aging Parents. Los Angeles: University of Southern California Press.

WENTOWSKI, G. J. (1981) "Reciprocity and the coping strategies of older people: cultural dimensions of network building." The Gerontologist 21: 600-609.

WHITE, D. and M. NEAL (1981) A Guidebook for the Family and Friends of Older Adults. Portland: Institute on Aging, Portland State University.

White House Conference on Aging Final Report (1981) Volume I. Washington, DC: Government Printing Office.

WOELFEL, J. (1976) "Communication across age levels," in H. J. Oyer and E. J. Oyer (eds.) Aging and Communication. Baltimore: University Park Press.

YAWNEY, B. A. and D. L. SLOVER (1973) "Relocation of the elderly." Social Work 18: 86-95.

ZARIT, S. H. (1980) Aging and Mental Disorders. New York: Free Press.

———— (1979) "The organic brain syndromes and family relationships," in P. K. Ragan (ed.) Aging Parents. Los Angeles: University of Southern California Press.

———— K. E. REEVER, and J. BACH-PETERSON (1980) "Relatives of the impaired elderly: correlates of feelings of burden." The Gerontologist 20: 649-655.

ABOUT THE AUTHORS

DIANNE SPRINGER received her master's of gerontological studies degree from Miami University, Oxford, Ohio. Currently she is employed as Central Manor Housing Manager and Director of the Personal Assistance Program for Greencroft, Inc., a retirement community in Goshen, Indiana. In this position she works closely with older adults and family caregivers. Prior to this, she was a gerontological social worker with the Elkhart County Council on Aging. There she co-led a support group for family caregivers, supervised the Pre-Admission Screening Program, and participated in a case management program.

TIMOTHY H. BRUBAKER is Associate Professor in the Department of Home Economics and Consumer Sciences and an Associate of the Family and Child Studies Center, Miami University, Oxford, Ohio. His research interests focus on family relationships in later life, attitudes toward the elderly, and service delivery to the elderly and their families. His articles have appeared in the *Journal of Gerontology, Research on Aging, Journal of Long Term Care Administration, The Family Coordinator,* and other scholarly journals. In 1983 he edited a book titled *Family Relationships in Later Life* (Sage Publications).